PRAISE FOR
TOUCHPOINT LEADERSHIP

"Leadership does not reside in leaders but in the relationships that leaders and followers create together to achieve a collective endeavour. Hilary Lines and Jacqui Scholes-Rhodes, two highly experienced leadership coaches, elucidate and illustrate with great insight what happens in the relationship at these points of meeting. They show how leaders can relate more effectively and what development and coaching can help them in this important task."

Peter Hawkins, author, Professor of Leadership at Henley Business School and Emeritus Chairman of Bath Consultancy Group

"Organizations function, for better or worse, through the interaction of the people who work there. In this book the authors focus on those touchpoints, and through their experience and insight show us that awareness of our own humanity is the vital spark which brings leadership to life."

Bill Knight OBE, former Senior Partner at Simmons & Simmons, Deputy Chairman of Council at Lloyd's of London and chairman of the Financial Reporting Review Panel

"Leaders... want to crack the code on how to have their teams fully engaged. The concepts and models in *Touchpoint Leadership* provide a fresh approach that will help leaders make sense of the world in which they operate and offer some different ideas on how they might proceed."

Gary Kildare, Global HR Officer at IBM Technology Solutions

Touchpoint Leadership

*For our children and grandchildren
and with gratitude to our parents who instilled
in us the value of relationships and curiosity*

Touchpoint
Leadership
Creating collaborative energy across teams and organizations

Hilary Lines and
Jacqui Scholes-Rhodes

KoganPage

LONDON PHILADELPHIA NEW DELHI

First published in Great Britain and the United States in 2013 by Kogan Page Limited

2nd Floor, 45 Gee Street
London EC1V 3RS
United Kingdom
www.koganpage.com

1518 Walnut Street, Suite 1100
Philadelphia PA 19102
USA

4737/23 Ansari Road
Daryaganj
New Delhi 110002
India

© Hilary Lines and Jacqui Scholes-Rhodes, 2013

The right of Hilary Lines and Jacqui Scholes-Rhodes to be identified as the authors of this work has been asserted by them in accordance with the Copyright, Designs and Patents Act 1988.

ISBN   978 0 7494 6578 0
E-ISBN   978 0 7494 6579 7

British Library Cataloguing-in-Publication Data

A CIP record for this book is available from the British Library.

Library of Congress Cataloging-in-Publication Data

Lines, Hilary.
   Touch point leadership : creating collaborative energy across teams and organizations / Hilary Lines, Jacqueline Scholes-Rhodes.
      p. cm.
   ISBN 978-0-7494-6578-0 – ISBN 978-0-7494-6579-7 (ebook)   1. Leadership.   2. Interpersonal relations.   3. Teams in the workplace.   I. Scholes-Rhodes, Jacqueline.   II. Title.
   HD57.7.L557 2013
   658.4'092–dc23
                                                                                                       2012039956

Typeset by Graphicraft Limited, Hong Kong
Printed and bound by CPI Group (UK) Ltd, Croydon, CR0 4YY

CONTENTS

OUR ETHICAL CODE

In writing this book we have aimed to illustrate the concept of Touchpoint Leadership in action, drawing on our work with leaders from a wide range of organizations and from across a diverse selection of sectors.

Our commitment to the confidentiality of our clients and research respondents is fundamental to our work and has been our first priority in selecting and shaping the examples to include in the book. To protect this confidentiality we have therefore developed stories in which a number of facts have been changed, and in some cases we have amalgamated more than one story, drawing out the generic learning pertinent to all touchpoint leaders rather than the specific insights experienced by the individual client. In the context of illustrating an aspect of Touchpoint Leadership, however, the meaning has been fully preserved.

In addition, we have contacted all those leaders whose stories have been adapted in this way and we have sought, and received, their express permission to incorporate the text into our book.

Hilary Lines
Jacqui Scholes-Rhodes

ACKNOWLEDGEMENTS

This book has emerged as we both look back on professional journeys spanning 30 years. It reflects our experience in coaching, advising and working alongside senior leaders and their teams during that period and it is enriched by our work with them. So first we want to acknowledge the contribution of our clients over the years to our learning, our thinking and to our growing sense of ourselves and our potential contribution. To protect their confidentiality, we refrain from naming them, but we thank each one of them, none the less.

On this journey, we have seldom travelled as 'sole traders'. In the past four years we have been fortunate in growing our learning partnership with each other, but there have been many other colleagues and mentors who have helped and guided us over the years and who have enriched our development. Many continue to do so. We cannot name them all, but Hilary would like to thank in particular Peter Hawkins, Keith Humphrey, Ian Griffiths, John Leary-Joyce, Nick Smith, David Dockray, Fran Johnston, Annie Mckee, Peninah Thomson, Andy Smith, Graham Lister and Kelvin Hard. Jacqui would like to recognize and appreciate Jack Whitehead, Peter Reason, Bill Torbert, Judi Marshall, Eden Charles, Ken Elvy, Kathy Woods and Jack MacPhail.

As we started gathering our thoughts and concepts for this book, a number of leaders gave generously of their time and shared their perspectives and their stories with us. Some kindly invited us to work with and alongside their teams to explore and test out the concept of Touchpoint Leadership in action. Again, our commitment to anonymity prevents us from naming them, but we are immensely grateful for their generosity and their wisdom.

We could not have completed this book without the dedication of Jacqui's husband, Jon. He brought us his technical skills, his eye for detail and his patience in creating figures and tables and in checking for internal consistency. And thanks, too, to Nick Lines for his unstinting support and to Joe, Harry and Tom Lines for putting up with blank looks and a spreading pile of books and papers during the past nine months.

Martina O' Sullivan, our publisher, has been a huge encouragement to us during the process of writing this book. Thank you Martina for your gentle guidance and challenge, and your spirit of optimism.

In building our concept and framework of Touchpoint Leadership we have drawn and built upon the research and approaches of many other writers and practitioners. We have aimed to acknowledge them throughout the book. We are aware, however, that in 30 years of experience, much of what we have absorbed may no longer be in the front of our consciousness. If we have failed to acknowledge others' work or have interpreted others' models incorrectly, we apologize. Please let us know and we will put it right. Thank you for giving us so much to build on.

Introduction

The way we communicate in the world has become so sophisticated, thanks to technology, but we often seem to forget that it is human beings that make companies work. For me, touchpoint is about getting back to basics: taking the time to think about who you need to connect with as a leader – not just those people you get on with – and thinking about how you want to come across so that you can relate to them as real people. **(FTSE 100 SENIOR EXECUTIVE, 2012)**

We agreed to write this book together because we're both curious and hopeful – curious about the vast potential that sits latent within the processes, structures and frameworks on which we build organizations, and at the same time hopeful that if we view organizations through a relationship lens we can create working environments that are both commercially successful and fulfilling for those who invest time and passion there.

Over the past 20 years we have worked increasingly with individual leaders, their teams and the leadership communities of local and global businesses to help address the challenge of working with the collective as a primary unit of change. We have worked with them to explore some of the behaviours and dialogues that can connect and disconnect leaders – from themselves, from each other and, more significantly, from the business outcomes they are targeting. We refer to it as a *three-tiered connectivity* – personal, interpersonal and organizational – and have found it essential in closely linking and aligning the success of each individual leader with the success of his or her teams and ultimately with the success of the business. This seems especially relevant in the early decades of the 21st century in the face of eroding trust in the governance of so many major institutions. And it is increasingly significant in a global world where we can be led to believe that technology keeps us permanently connected – only to find that when partnership and alliance is critical to success we have not in fact developed the quality of relationship that is needed to grow and sustain our connectivity.

Standing back from the challenges facing senior leaders in an increasingly complex, diverse and interconnected world, we started to explore the following questions:

- *What if* leaders were able to work at the very point of difference between people – the touchpoint – and explore the positive qualities of relationships that can be built on healthy tension and friction?

- *What if* they were to develop the self and interpersonal awareness necessary to develop and grow those touchpoints more consciously and adeptly and therefore create collaboration rather than division and fall-out at the point of difference between people and groups?

- *What if* whole organizations could join up the positive energy and creativity of networks of relationships – and somehow drive out the diminishing and potentially destructive qualities of unreconciled difference?

These are deliberately challenging questions, and we know they are not easy to answer. It was in fact these challenges that led us to develop the concept and developmental framework of Touchpoint Leadership – and we therefore ask you to hold them lightly as you read the book, noticing what other questions arise that have relevance for your own business.

The Touchpoint Leadership proposition

Touchpoint Leadership is founded on the belief that relationships are the primary unit of value in organizations and that for enterprises to be healthy, effective and immensely rewarding leaders need to put relationships at the heart of everything they do. It is through these relationships that they can help generate and sustain positive energy at the point at which people connect. We refer to these points of connection as the *touchpoints*.

We have built a developmental framework of Touchpoint Leadership based on three domains, summarized in Figure 0.1. This framework and its underlying principles have been built from our experience of working with leaders who have themselves invested in developing touchpoints across their organizations as a means of building connected and creative enterprises. Throughout the book we draw on these client experiences to illustrate the domains in action.

FIGURE 0.1   Touchpoint Leadership: summary, definition and framework

Touchpoint Leadership is the capacity of a leader to ignite positive energy at the critical points of interaction and difference between people and groups in an organization, for the benefit of the enterprise as a whole.

To develop Touchpoint Leadership capability, a leader needs to focus on three developmental domains:

Personal:

- The ability to bring his full self to interactions with others.
  This requires him to develop self-awareness, relational agility and a clear moral compass, often through a process of deep reflection. We refer to this as Domain One: Priming the touchpoint.

Interpersonal:

- The ability to attend to what happens at the moment of connection with others – the touchpoint itself – adapting his presence and behaviour to ignite energy, affirm difference and to catalyse mutual learning. We refer to this as Domain Two: Connecting to ignite energy and co-creation at the touchpoint.

Organizational:

- The ability to take a systemic view of the connections that need to be made to build collective value, in order to engender learning and collaboration across the enterprise as a whole. This is Domain Three: Building and sustaining the collaborative enterprise.

In the chapters that follow we illustrate how important it is that touchpoint leaders remain permanently at their learning edge, constantly reflecting on and exploring how they can bring their whole selves into their leadership roles. We share the insights we have gained from helping leaders construct meaning from the complexity within which they operate, engaging dialogically with the rich mix of values, beliefs, strengths, emotional and physical resonance implicit in the diversity of their organizations. And we evidence how friction often arises from the difference encountered at the touchpoint – between people, groups and business communities – and how we have worked with clients to transform this energy into a source of sustainable growth.

We use extracts from our client stories to demonstrate how taking an integrated and systemic approach to building relationships can catalyse a very powerful and connective means of enhancing an organization's capacity to grow and adapt in response to both current and emerging business issues. We demonstrate how the quality of these connections can both liberate talent – especially at a time when we know that this is an organizational issue – and engender a form of relational leadership that can support and catalyse the quality of partnership that is so critical to operating in today's global market. Fluid boundaries and the increasing complexity of our global structures signal that these connecting qualities can occur both within the organization and in the spaces on the outside of its boundaries, and in most cases will include our clients, suppliers and local stakeholders.

The benefits of Touchpoint Leadership

The book is primarily written for those business leaders who are looking for new perspectives on unlocking the capacity for innovation and growth in their businesses. These leaders understand the value of personal development and teamwork, they have probably thought long and hard about their own leadership and have themselves gained value from high quality development interventions. And yet they are looking for something new – a different lens and set of tools with which they can release the collective potential of their teams, their colleagues, their whole business.

Many of these leaders increasingly need to read their organizations as an integrated whole – focusing on global connection and diversity, encouraging collaboration, distributed accountability, partnering and collective ownership. They may also be facing intractable dilemmas on a personal front: how to reconcile the incessant demands of a top job with the need for a more rounded life, for personal health, family life, connection to their community, friendship. Caught between 'home team' and 'away team' they are possibly finding that neither is fully functional, while at the same time recognizing that their organizations cannot continue to expect more and more from individuals and that the shift must come from the collective.

The book will also be of interest to those human resources leaders who are dealing with the growing challenges of integration and connection across complex structures and increasing diversity. As they explore ways of connecting divisional needs to corporate mission and strategy, of connecting individual development needs to organizational opportunities, and of connecting the talent and value brought by diverse groups with the needs of the whole business, this book will offer a new lens through which to view their integrating role. It will offer support by providing approaches to affirm and strengthen their impact on the systems in which they play a vital part, whether operating from a central community of expertise or operating in a business partner role embedded within the business.

And finally, the world is currently littered with examples of businesses, financial institutions and governments that are either crumbling or have crumbled largely because of a lack of relational leadership, a lack of connection between the external and internal worlds of governance and control, and a lack of connection between the individual passions and actions of those leading and those being led. As we noted above, trust has been lost in many major institutions and sustained and positive social change is now concerned with the creation of systems that will benefit the greater good. That means a new focus on developing connections and relationships that will promote understanding and dialogue, and help affirm the difference that can be so catalytic in learning and challenging the status quo.

We believe therefore that this book will have a readership beyond purely businesses, and will include those who are both involved in and interested in wider social change.

About this book

How we have written this book

Writing the book has proved to be a dynamic process, our work and conversations with clients generating new questions that we subsequently included in our ongoing inquiry. Some of these inquiries were formalized as workshops with a selected group of leaders, the paradoxical challenges of connection and difference very pertinent to their businesses. We have also been able to maintain an organic form to the book – sharing, as co-authors, the dialogues of both our collective and separate work, and allowing our own differences as well as our similarities to be heard. Some of the evidence of the touchpoints of our own writing partnership shows through in our shared stories, our different perspectives of action research and principles of Gestalt shaping our individual work.

Our coming together to write this book as a partnership has given us a unique opportunity, therefore, to explore the nature of relationship as we work together. United by an area of common interest and experience, and a philosophy of human behaviour and change, we made some early assumptions about the fact that we were 'talking about the same thing'. However, early in our four-year relationship we became fascinated by the differences in the perspectives we were bringing to this subject. Sometimes our dialogue seemed to become blocked by difference – of language, assumption and outlook, and the task seemed insurmountable ... soon to be followed by a freeing up, a meeting of minds, the source of the liberation hidden to us.

This led us to the idea that we would use our own dialogue as research data in this book – and give you, the reader, the opportunity to catch a glimpse of the way our own dialogue has progressed. Throughout the text we therefore share the questions that have been so generative in developing our own and others' understanding of

Touchpoint Leadership, and invite you to pause and consider your own leadership challenges through a similar relational lens as you select the chapters most relevant to you and your business.

Book structure and signposting

We are aware that the different chapters and sections of the book will appeal to different readers, depending on your role, area of interest and your learning style. To help you navigate we offer the following guidance.

In Chapter 1 we set out in full the concept and developmental framework of Touchpoint Leadership, evidencing how we've drawn on the very practical experiences of our client work and showing how our work relates to the practices and writings of other researchers. In Chapter 2 we focus on the preparation needed by individual leaders to deepen their self-awareness as a way of developing the qualities of attention that are needed at the touchpoint. We refer to this as 'priming the touchpoint', and share the stories of individual leaders as they explore the impact of their presence and relational capacity in their current and future roles.

In Chapters 3 to 5 we explore a range of case studies drawn from a wide spectrum of clients to illustrate Touchpoint Leadership in action. Chapter 3 examines pivotal relationships of power and trust, sharing insights into the positive impact of shared leadership while also highlighting how a loss of energy can occur if the touchpoint between two people is not fully collaborative. Chapter 4 focuses on the nature of partnership, sharing examples of our work with major professional services firms and exploring how brand identity takes on meaning at the touchpoint with the client. Chapter 5 explores the possibilities that are often left latent in the middle leadership layers of organizations – and the potential gulf that can open up between the intent of the 'top' leaders as they become disconnected from the energies and potentiality of the 'middles'. We also stand back and reflect on the organization as a whole, putting forward the proposition that Touchpoint Leadership is essential in helping co-create the collaborative enterprise, built on a connective capacity to learn and a level of trust that gives permission to act freely.

In our final chapter – Chapter 6 – we provide areas for exploration to help readers work towards their own touchpoint mastery, inviting them to continue to view leadership through a relational lens, using the principles of Touchpoint Leadership as a way of exploring the huge potential we know exists at the point at which individuals begin to connect.

The case for Touchpoint Leadership

01

> "In organisations, real power and energy is generated through relationships (and) the patterns of relationships and the capacities to form them are more important than tasks, functions, roles and positions. (MARGARET WHEATLEY, LEADERSHIP AND THE NEW SCIENCE, 1992)

The leadership challenge – and the paradoxes

As we move through the second decade of the 21st century both private and public sector leaders face increasingly complex challenges and hard choices. They need to engage diffuse and diverse workforces across multiple cultures and belief systems; they are expected to find ever more creative ways to stimulate growth while cutting costs; they recognize the need to engage each new generation of leaders anxious to live out their different priorities and values; and they are driven by the need to foster innovation and competitive edge in a complex and constrained world where regulation, governance and sustainability are core concerns. Add to these the failures of leadership and governance in the financial world in the first decade of the century, and the seemingly intractable problems of creating and distributing wealth across the world, and we recognize that there are significant signs that something in leadership needs to change.

Writers in the field of leadership emphasize that the time for the hero leader is past and that skills in team leadership and collaboration are now paramount. As early as 1984 Bradford and Cohen[1] identified the aspirations of hero leaders as untenable and unhealthy, and tracked the detrimental effect on organizational performance. In their subsequent work they termed the phrase 'post-heroic leader' to identify a new genre of leader who would engage collaboratively and have the courage to seek answers from others.[2] Joiner and Josephs[3] built on the characteristics of the 'post-heroic leader' through their work on 'leadership agility' in 2007, demonstrating a growing focus on interdependency and commitment to collaborative relationships rooted in a deep sense of shared purpose.

At the end of the 1990s Daniel Goleman[4] and others stressed the importance of leaders being able to generate emotional connection with their people, and evidenced a direct relationship between leadership, organizational climate and business performance. As we progress through the century, and our capacity to connect through social networking, video conferencing, Twitter and the like appears to increase daily, our need to connect *relationally* becomes even more important. But there is a paradox: as the technology speeds up our communication and its global reach expands our capacity to communicate globally, the structures and behaviours on which we build our organizations fail to keep pace – and instead of leveraging what the new technologies have made possible we risk becoming overloaded by the very richness that makes them so enticing. Psychologists have pointed to the evidence that the younger generation's increasing use of social networking to form and conduct relationships is helping to create a generation of people who have not honed the skills for relating person-to-person 'in the real world' or, as Carr[5] proposes in his work, may even be re-defining what the 'real world' means to them as a result of the impact internet technology use has on the functioning of the brain.

As businesses continue to extend over global boundaries and build increasingly complex structures of joint ventures, partnering agreements, third party and associate deals, we are noticing that their success is depending more and more on their capacity to build and work through their relationships. Many leaders are already beginning to focus on their capacity for dialogue, collaboration, teamworking and an ability to leverage a growing network of power structures. They recognize that for creative energy to feed these new businesses they will need to know how to facilitate its flow and to recognize where it has been allowed to become blocked and even dry up.

We also observe that as alliances and partnerships become part of the organizational model business leaders are recognizing that they need to grow their capacity to read their organizations as an integrated whole and above all to find ways to engage the many and diverse groups that make up their organizations. Such leaders know that the huge effort they put into organizational transformation must be sustained over time and in a way that enables their own leaders to work with the emergent and changing nature of the business. The capacity to learn, to adapt and to flex is essential.

We witness through our development work the stress being experienced by many senior leaders who are striving to make a difference in such a challenging environment. While we see many organizations recognizing that younger entrants to the workforce are less attracted to the lifelong, 24/7 work and career patterns of earlier generations, we also note that these issues are of increasing concern to senior leaders. We see signs of a reluctance to step into senior leadership roles, including CEO roles, the reluctance based on an assumption that the demands of the role must necessarily demand the separation of a 'leader self' from 'whole self'. This disconnection is sometimes seen as a price too high to pay and challenges those in the succession pools and high-potential development groups to question whether the cost of devoting their whole life, in terms of time and of purpose and value, is just too high a price to pay. Boyatzis and McKee[6] speak of the 'sacrifice syndrome' that can develop for senior leaders whose absorption in their work at the expense of attention to their health, their personal life and their psychological and spiritual wellbeing puts them in a place of deficit and ill health. This has a disruptive impact for the individuals, their families and for the organizations they lead, and it raises a significant question for these leaders: how can they enrich their sense of meaning and purpose in their work, maintain a rewarding balance between work and other life commitments, *and* work with the pace and complexity required in the modern business world?

Those leading international businesses have access to an increasingly diverse pool of human talent with which to conduct business.

While this diversity offers greater potential in terms of variety of skill, perspective and creativity, and deepens the richness of our life experience, it also adds to the complexity and ambiguity in human relationships at work. In our consulting work we are constantly struck by the ability of organizations to recruit for difference and then reject the very thing they have sought. Ibarra and Hansen[7] share the same reflections in their work on collaborative leadership and refer to the inordinate costs of attracting talented employees only to subject them to 'homogenizing processes that kill creativity'. Research shows that the envisioned benefits of merger and acquisition are often not realized because of the failure to embrace and nourish the very difference that was the attractor in the first place.

It appears that human beings may value difference but also fear its impact on them and their way of doing things. Maybe this is why the issues of engagement never seem to be fully resolved, and why gender diversity on boards progresses at such a slow pace in many countries of the world. The reality is that while processes can help in all these things, no real change is achieved unless we look at deeper attitudinal factors that stop us from releasing our human need for control and homogeneity and instead develop our ability to embrace the breadth and diversity of the contrasting skills and styles that others bring.

We offer the concept of Touchpoint Leadership as a way of helping leaders navigate this complexity by focusing on relationships as the primary unit of energy and value in their business, and attending to how they enable themselves and others to build constructive relationships through the many points of connection – the touchpoints – in their working lives.

Seeing leadership through a new lens: the Touchpoint Leadership proposition

To take a relational, joined up approach to leading their businesses, leaders will need to maximize rather than minimize the difference within their organizations and across key inter-organizational boundaries.

Against the backdrop of broken trust, greater governance and control, and significant questions about the morality of leadership, we have been asked increasingly by leaders to work with them to help rebuild energy and confidence in their organizations. We have worked with the challenges of engaging distributed workforces, the incessant demands of centralized leadership, the turmoil of constant change – and in each case our experience has consistently shown that organizations can only realize their full potential if they transform the connections between the people, teams and sub-units that make up their business system.

It is this work that has led us to develop a new lens on the role of leadership, putting the focus firmly on the connections that enable individuals, teams and whole organizations to work and learn together. Our Touchpoint Leadership development framework is founded on the following beliefs.

Leaders have the opportunity to unlock energy, creativity and learning every day, through the quality of their own points of connection with individuals, teams and groups. Touchpoint Leadership means focusing on those points of connection that will engender new insights, free up creativity and encourage challenge in a way that contributes to *mutual learning and growth.*

Leaders must attend to the *points of difference* between people, groups and business communities in order to *optimize the value of the relationships* that connect them. This difference is a vital and rich source of learning, and fundamental to optimizing business value.

Leaders also have the opportunity to *ignite collective energy* across the organization, in ways that can transform productivity and performance.

Leaders need to *trust individuals to act freely and responsibly* – supporting the acceptance and expression of the individual and collective vulnerability that are fundamental to learning, and helping suspend habitual responses and actions so that new realities can emerge.

This focus on connection is fundamental to Touchpoint Leadership, and illustrations throughout the book will show how it has helped bridge the gulf that can emerge between executive and middle management levels, between critical executive relationships at the top, between divisions in the same organization and across external and internal client/customer relationships.

In the vignettes that follow we illustrate how two individual leaders came to understand that the real work they needed to do lay in the development of their relationships with others, and particularly those 'others' with whom they did not naturally connect. It was at the point of connection with the people in their business – particularly those whose motivation they impacted, those whom they avoided or those they came into conflict with – that they could begin to maximize the collective value of the business and start to build a contribution that far exceeded anything they could achieve alone.

CASE STUDY

David had previously worked in a large-scale public sector organization where spending time in conversation was considered 'swanning about'. He like many thousands of others was directed and rewarded to achieve outcomes – tangible, measurable and within the required timescales. He'd been very successful, and had helped launch a new and quite innovative alternative to part of the service delivery portfolio.

In his new role, in a small start-up, he was expected to demonstrate the same drive for innovation and delivery, but he was failing to have an impact. He understood the challenge fully, and could articulate the contribution he was meant to make, but he could not understand how to bring his colleagues with him. He was beginning to show signs of derailment and was losing the confidence to continue.

During his coaching sessions we explored his notion of 'swanning about' – and helped him examine the options open to him in a small, entrepreneurial firm where relationships were key to success. Up to that point he had considered relationships 'nice to have', something he nurtured in his spare time. Gradually he realized that relationships were in fact key to his success – he had to connect with others through their energy and passion for the business to ensure they worked in partnership with him. Investing time in conversation was pivotal to his role.

CASE STUDY

Barbara was a CEO of a technology business. She came to coaching because she had received feedback about being remote and somewhat abrupt in her interactions with others. One day in our coaching conversations she said with irritation: 'Companies don't want people just to talk to each other – they want them to get things done!' We went on to explore what it would be like if she saw organizations as, in reality, a series of relationships and talking to people as *the* work.

These two clients saw clearly the changes they needed to make – and made them. But we continue to encounter the negative impact of leaders failing to make pivotal connections across their organizations, in some cases manifested in their struggles to engage whole professional communities in critical change programmes, and in some painfully evident in the breakdown of the relationships at board level, including the partnership of chair and CEO.

This ability of people and teams to destroy, as opposed to create, value at their touchpoint of connection is illustrated in Figure 1.1. The 'vicious cycle' in the diagram shows how a potentially damaging cycle can occur when the trust between two people or groups breaks down. The example is based on an environment that encourages individual competition, in which an individual's need to succeed triggers a personal fear of failure. If the environment also values individual over collective excellence, and the level of trust between individuals and teams is poor, this can lead to the individual protecting and isolating him or herself. As this isolation increases, he or she may start to attribute negative intent to others, further increasing organizational fragmentation and having a consequent negative impact on morale and performance. This is likely to go unchecked without intervention in the cycle.

Trust is essential in helping break this cycle, and in 2012 the UK's Chartered Institute of Personnel and Development commissioned a report on the state of trust, describing trust as an ability to accept

FIGURE 1.1 Catalysing a virtuous – and vicious – cycle at the touchpoint

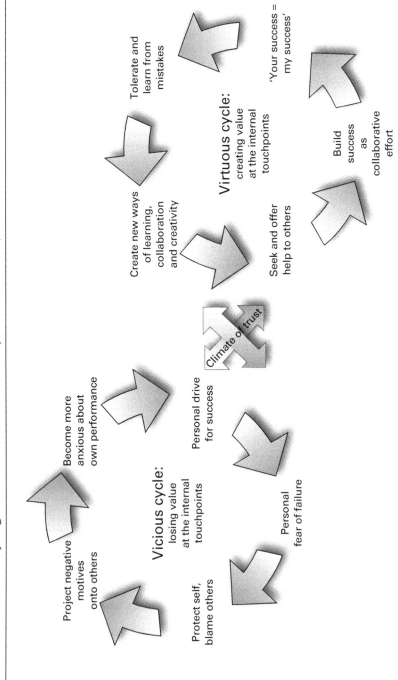

'a certain amount of *uncertainty* but being willing to take risks and go into the unknown because you trust that the other party will act in a positive way towards you. So it is about a willingness to make oneself vulnerable in the face of uncertainty or insecurity'[8]. Once a climate of trust is developed and maintained, individuals within the system feel able and confident enough to ask for and offer help,[9] achievements grow from interdependent rather than purely independent action, and the potential emerges for a climate of collaboration and connection that helps achieve results that would otherwise be out of reach.[10] The 'virtuous cycle' in Figure 1.1 illustrates this.

Leaders have the power and capacity to determine which way the relationship dynamics flow in this interconnected cycle through their attention to the touchpoints between themselves and others in their organizations. In fact, taking responsibility for these touchpoint connections is a sign of being prepared to take on the role of the leader in an organizational system. But in the hectic everyday life of most people this central role can be underplayed or ignored, resulting in a huge waste of human potential.

The three domains of Touchpoint Leadership

In this section we look more closely at what it takes to develop the capacity for Touchpoint Leadership, setting out the core concepts within a framework of three domains which we describe as:

1 *Priming the touchpoint to become relational.* Viewing the challenges of developing Touchpoint Leadership from an individual leader perspective, exploring how a leader personally prepares and develops the capacity for creating the conditions for positive connections with others. The focus is on developing self-awareness, relational agility and a clear moral compass.

2 *Igniting connective energy at the touchpoint.* Exploring what happens at the touchpoint itself, as individuals, teams and groups come together in the spirit of co-creation. This puts

the focus on developing a capacity to ignite energy, affirm difference and catalyse mutual growth, which in turn delivers exponential value at the client, team and business partner interfaces.

3 *Building the collaborative enterprise.* Standing back and looking at the organization as a whole, noticing the wider dynamics that impact on every touchpoint connection and play a significant role in enabling a culture of learning and collaboration. The focus here is on connecting to engage, co-creating learning systems and building trust.

In this chapter we draw on brief illustrations from our work with leaders, teams and organizations to help illustrate the domains in action. We also signpost the sections of the book where they are illustrated and developed further. We refer to the research and writing of others in the field of leadership and business coaching and psychology to demonstrate how we have developed Touchpoint Leadership as both an extension of current leadership practice and as a unique way of integrating personal, relational and organizational insights. And we evidence how the domains can be used as a structured approach to developing Touchpoint Leadership across a range of interventions, sometimes working with individual leaders as they seek to increase their impact and in other cases engaging whole professional communities in exploring the pivotal relationships that will be critical to their collective performance. As you read it our invitation to you is to:

- Reconsider your leadership through the lens of relationships and the connections between people, and deepen your understanding of how your leadership could change to enhance the quality of connection across the organizations you lead, and the development path that will be most valuable to you.

- Understand the dilemmas you face as a leader, your own reactions to them and how, by embracing difference, you could help liberate creativity, talent and potential in your business.

- Adopt an integrated and systemic approach to your leadership that offers a powerful and connective means of enhancing your organization's capacity to grow and adapt in response to both current and emerging business issues.

We set out the key elements of each of the three domains in Figure 1.2. The touchpoint itself is represented by domain 2, sitting at the centre of the diagram and illustrating how each touchpoint has the potential to ignite energy, affirm difference and catalyse mutual growth. The domains represented by triangles either side of the touchpoint illustrate how the individual qualities of connection, and the network of connections created across the enterprise, converge at each touchpoint – the impact of the touchpoint therefore being felt both singly and collectively. The lower triangle, domain 1, is built on the individual leader's personal insights into his or her 'life narrative', priming the touchpoint with purpose, a readiness to learn and remain vulnerable, and a capacity to engage dialogically. The upper triangle, domain 3, represents the leader's capacity to create an organization that is able and willing to learn, to make connections happen where

FIGURE 1.2   The concept of Touchpoint Leadership

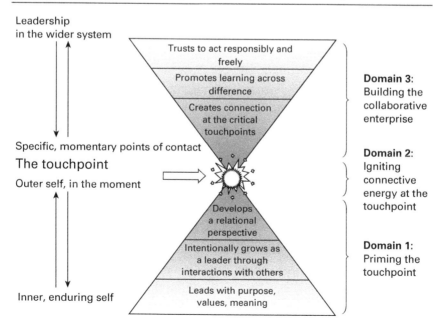

they are critical for business value, and a capacity to trust individuals to act consequentially and responsibly. This is Touchpoint Leadership in action, co-creating a collaborative and productive enterprise.

The three domains in detail

Domain 1: Priming the touchpoint to become relational

In priming the touchpoint a leader:

- Develops a deep appreciation of his or her own and the organization's purpose and values, and holds him or herself firmly accountable to these principles.
- Is prepared to be vulnerable in his or her interactions with others so that he or she intentionally and consciously grows as a leader.
- Is able to see him or herself through a relational lens, can discern the patterns that influence his or her ability to co-create value at the touchpoint.

In this first domain of Touchpoint Leadership we use the word 'priming' as a way of describing how leaders might change the very nature of the attention they bring to their leadership, developing what we refer to as a 'relational lens' that helps them see the world as a series of connecting threads and relationships, and puts the emphasis firmly on their capacity to connect. This relational leadership is characterized by the reciprocal qualities of: engaging dialogically, learning through and with others, and being adept at rewriting the personal narratives that make up the leader's sense of 'self'. This is covered in more detail in Chapter 2.

We also encourage leaders to realize the power implicit in developing a depth of self-awareness that enables them to be fully present at the touchpoint – confident, certain and clear in direction – and yet at the same time vulnerable, curious and open to changes in their knowing.[11] We encourage leaders to notice how much they can learn and change through their interactions, each touchpoint an opportunity to reflect, extract new meaning and subsequently change the dynamic. This means remaining constantly in touch with the detail being played out at the touchpoint, noticing the patterns of exchange, the impact of an individual intervention and being prepared to acknowledge not knowing when that in itself can have significant influence on the outcome.

Bringing value and meaning to the organization by remaining grounded in a deep appreciation of own purpose and values, and holding oneself firmly accountable to these principles Like many leadership practitioners we support the premise that those leading others need to have a level of confidence that inspires and engages. But we also believe that this confidence must be built on a grounding of deep awareness of personal values, an awareness of how those values in turn impact personal meaning-making, and the capacity to articulate this grounding as a set of guiding principles that serve as a moral compass to which the leader must be prepared to hold him or herself to account. We refer to this as being 'fully present' at the touchpoint.

We therefore focus on leaders' capacity to connect with those deeply held values and beliefs that give meaning to their leadership – articulating what it means for them personally to lead the business and then encouraging them to take a critical view from the perspective of colleagues, stakeholders and clients. In some cases this will cause a constructive tension or paradox[12] – a 'living contradiction'[13] – as leaders realize the fundamental differences that exist between their personal values and goals and those of the organization. The individual leader's moral compass emerges from these dialogues – as does the source of his or her energy and motivation.

We have already said that Touchpoint Leadership is built on the premise that difference can have a generative impact on an organization's ability to learn and grow, and that by remaining alert and open to learning we have the capacity to both strengthen our individual identities and capacities as leaders *and* reinforce our difference. This avoids the risk of 'smoothing over', described by Judi Marshall[14] in her work on women managers as a 'dysfunctional communion strategy', warning that it can become a form of self-distortion and suppression.

To do this we first work with leaders to help them fully realize their own difference, encouraging them to bring their 'true' self into their leadership roles. We are aware that theories of 'real self' and 'authentic leadership' continue to multiply and so it's important that we differentiate the meaning of 'true self' in the context of Touchpoint Leadership. We share Rowan's (2001)[15] proposition that the 'real self' would be better described as an experience rather than a theoretical construct – encouraging leaders to reflect on how it *feels* to be *whole*, to be *in flow*. And we are keen to encourage leaders to think of themselves as fully present – avoiding any distortion in the way in which they might be showing up. When we do meet the self-image or the sub-personality muscling in on the leader's space then we encourage some straight talking! Other authors have used the term 'authentic leadership' as a way of encouraging individuals to lead, behave and relate in a way that is aligned to their personal values, and in his work George[16] describes the importance of such an approach to leadership by exploring how it can help engender trust and genuine connection. This authenticity has to have legitimacy and meaning when subjected to the critical appraisal of colleagues, stakeholders, clients – and the market as a whole. Without this systemic connection we may run the risk of encountering a CEO who cannot see beyond his or her blind spot – or a chair who has lost the ability to challenge with impact as he or she's become overly vested in his or her personal values of homogeneity and harmony.

We also know that few senior executives allow themselves this space to reflect deeply on what matters most to them, a view echoed by Boyatzis and McKee[17] in their work on resonant leadership. They illustrate how the pressured work roles of many senior executives can lead them to lose their sense of purpose in life, causing them to become detached from what is important to them and, consequently, from those they are attempting to lead.

Borrowing the term from Schon (1991)[18] we therefore work with leaders to become 'reflective practitioners', encouraging them to connect with their personal stories as a means of building new insights into the way in which they are present as leaders. The inquiry framework we offer in Chapter 6 is built on this approach. Rosenwald and Ochberg[19] describe how the telling and retelling of stories in this way can help generate new meaning, and in Chapter 2 we share stories of clients who have done just this – rewriting their narratives as a way of reconnecting with values, experiences and insights that for whatever reason have become distorted or lost over time. We are not alone in using narratives in this way. In her work on the 'democratic enterprise', Gratton[20] refers to this kind of reflective development as 'life narratives', in which leaders are encouraged to piece together what might at first appear to be disparate actions before they find the thread that will pull them together into a cohesive picture. In all of these cases the insights drawn from the experiences have been used to help make new sense of the experiences underpinning each leader's theory of leadership.

Leaders have the opportunity to release an immense energy when they take time to share the passions they bring to their work, to articulate the true legacy that they want to leave in the business and the values that they want to lead by. We refer to these as 'the values that create anchors for action'. Our own experience of helping clients find sustaining energy for their leadership has shown the importance of being able to stand back from the work schedule and look with new eyes, a new frame and new emotional awareness, enabling them to see how far their current behaviour is contributing to – or detracting from – what they really want to achieve in the world, both in and outside the workplace. In the two following examples we illustrate how two separate clients were able to do just this.

CASE STUDY

We were supporting an industrial chemicals business undergo a major transformation aimed at radically enhancing its business effectiveness. The client had commissioned us to help engage all levels of management in designing the way in which the future organization would look and feel after the major changes had been achieved. People appeared to be engaged, giving all outward signs of being energetic and generating ideas. But there were constant niggles and complaints outside of meetings, an underlying sense of irritation and frustration being expressed by the management group sitting one level below the executive team, which spoke of unease and fear of change. It was clear that the programme had so far not captured the hearts of these managers.

Working closely with the MD and executive team, we first helped them explore in depth what this change meant to them. What kind of business would it enable them to create? How would this help them achieve their own aspirations as senior leaders? What hopes and values underpinned these ambitions? We then brought the whole senior management group together for a two-day workshop aimed at enabling them to explore how, through their own leadership, they could build a creative and productive working culture throughout the redesigned business. It was vital that this workshop helped them generate the positive energy needed for them to engage others.

As soon as the MD started to speak at the opening of the meeting, we knew that the energy would be there. Speaking quietly, with passion and conviction, the MD talked of his personal commitment to this business, of the values that he inherited from his father, and of the legacy he was determined to leave in this business. The soul had been breathed into this programme of change and the next two days were alive with a spirit of collaboration and open commitment.

CASE STUDY

Terry was an ambitious and successful sales executive in a major multinational, admired for his business-building capability. He loved his work and was never happier than when he was working at the customer interface. He gradually became aware, however, that he was losing touch with his family life because of his extensive travel. He described how, on a recent business trip, he had met, in an airport lounge, his ex-boss whom he held in very high regard. Philip, in his 50s, was now a millionaire, but despite his financial success, was still spending most of his life travelling on business. Terry noticed an air of tiredness and stress in him and it seemed that his personal life was not in good shape. 'I love the work I do but I do not want to be like Philip,' Terry told us.

As he reflected, Terry realized that the potential to change his life lay in his reaction to his clients and his senior colleagues as they asked him to get involved in more and more things. His inability to say 'no' to new client opportunities was impacting on the way he was relating with his children and wife. It became clear to him that if he changed his behaviour he could fulfil his ambition for a successful career *and* have a fulfilling family life. To do this he explored how he could break out of his knee-jerk 'yes' response to all requests from senior managers to take on more work. As he did this, he saw that growing his ability to say 'no' had the potential to help him grow his leadership authority and presence, and to find a way to communicate his values to his own team.

The capacity to intentionally and consciously grow as a leader: being prepared to be vulnerable in interactions with others Having talked about confidence being critical to a leader's ability to inspire and engage we also put the focus firmly on sustaining a quality of vulnerability. By that we mean a vulnerability that is both courageous and safe, bringing a quality of humility to the touchpoint that enables the leader to learn with and through others in a way that also engages others in the process. We refer to it in Chapter 2 as a leader's 'curiosity and perseverance to be permanently at their learning edge' and in the following story illustrate how two clients found the experience quite catalytic in enabling changes that they might not otherwise have achieved.

CASE STUDY

A CEO of an international business had become concerned about his IT director. The latter was highly experienced in the industry and had been a valued member of the executive team for a number of years, but in the past two years some mistakes had been made for which the CEO held this director accountable. As a result of disagreement between the two of them concerning the root cause of these problems, their relationship had deteriorated to the point of avoidance. The CEO knew that unless he took some action more problems would arise and that the IT director would either leave or he would require him to leave. It would have been easy in some ways to hasten the termination discussion, but the CEO knew of the capability of this man, and also had enough humility to know that this issue was not just down to one person's 'fault'. He knew that it also lay in the quality of the relationship between them. He decided to invest time in a process that would enable each of them to stand back and learn what was really going on for the other, and how this was impacting on their ability to work together.

Through individual coaching, they each started to see how their own styles were stopping them from seeking contributions from the other and learning from them. The discomfort that they both felt from their conversations was feeding a pattern of avoidance which in turn was reinforcing a lack of mutual understanding. The first paired coaching session demonstrated how far the two directors were prepared to make themselves vulnerable in front of the other for the sake of a better relationship – the awkwardness in the room was palpable. Slowly they started to share that they had come to appreciate how their own behaviour was hindering collaboration – and also to provide feedback to the other about what they needed from them to be more open and cooperative. With each small step the conversation became less stilted, more fluid.

Through their willingness to be vulnerable and to learn from the limits of their own perceptions and capabilities, the CEO and IT director were able to encourage each other to address what was blocking their relationship. This enabled them to develop a way of working in which each could learn from the other to build a spirit of collaboration in support of the business.

Maintaining this level of vulnerability relies on high levels of trust and respect, and later in the book we share an example of one CEO who took enormous risks when he put himself into a position of 'not knowing' – clearing the space for his executives to engage dialogically with him but far too soon for any of them to respond immediately. He was offering them his readiness to develop a shared sense of meaning and ownership together – his vulnerability clear to the whole organization as he admitted that he did not have the answers. Their vulnerability was evident in their inability to respond, and their discomfort at not knowing initially blocked the insights and learning that the CEO had anticipated.

And so we have another paradox at the touchpoint – new insights can only emerge if the individuals involved can let go of their certainties, release their grip on the 'knowledge' that has served them so well in the past and learn the value of 'knowing' in the here and now. This is very clearly illustrated in Chapter 4 where we explore some of the challenges that arose in a professional partnership firm as they wrestled with the tension of being expert, while also valuing the insights drawn from the touchpoint itself, which in their case was the client interface.

So we encourage leaders to *value the insights of vulnerability*. This is not to say that leaders should not expect to deliver their own views and of course many look to leaders for clarity and direction. There are also some who might argue that a propensity to learn from others smacks of weakness, or an over-democratic approach. Without a strong sense of 'self' we would probably agree, but the touchpoint leader holds the 'certainty' of knowing who he or she is as a leader, in the here and now, and so can be both vulnerable and strong in 'not knowing'. And he or she remains anchored in a process of continuously learning.

Developing a relational perspective, engendering qualities of dialogic engagement to co-create value at the touchpoint In this third sub-domain the leader develops a new quality of engagement at the touchpoint, suspending judgement in a way that allows mutual insights to emerge and engaging in a form of creative exchange that can enable both personal and collective transformation. This concept of a 'light touch' connection was developed by Jacqui Scholes-Rhodes in 2002,[21] drawing on the work of both Isaacs[22] and Bohm[23] on dialogue. In Chapter 2 we show how we have further refined her original seven principles of 'dialogic inquiry' to develop the four principles of reciprocal engagement that help define Touchpoint Leadership.

This form of exchange catalyses a quality of mutual learning and growth and opens up the ability of a leader to create a space in which questions are valued and encouraged. This space can become an opportunity to consider what has individual and shared meaning and, when extended to the whole enterprise, begins to create very new possibilities for engagement that are both sustainable and built on deeply personal values.

As leaders develop insight into the way in which they make sense of the world, articulating assumptions and beliefs that both construct and deconstruct their ability to connect, we work with them to help observe how this lands with others, drawing on the work of Goleman[24] on the importance of self, interpersonal and social awareness in enabling the leader to connect emotionally with people to create a climate conducive to productive engagement.[25] We take note of the energy that is catalysed by their leadership – and we help raise awareness of where it might actually drain energy, and the type of dialogic engagement that they need to apply to help value the difference in the room. The following vignette provides an illustration.

CASE STUDY

The leader of the team was a highly compassionate person who believed strongly in the development of his people. He had very high expectations of them and cared deeply about how they made the best of themselves in their work with clients. His behaviour, however, rather than expressing his belief in people, sometimes expressed his frustration in the way they performed and acted. This led them to distance themselves from him – which then fed an increasingly negative impression of them in his mind, and a deepened loss of confidence in his team members. It was not until he had taken the time to stand back from his day-to-day work and deepen his awareness of how he impacted on people that he was able to intentionally shift the way in which he interacted with them. As he explored with his team how he impacted on them, this leader began to see, as if in slow motion, the moment when his emotions created a touchpoint in which his team members felt undermined. He started to experiment with ways of holding his opinions more lightly and curiously, to allow more mutual exchange through the interaction. This helped him develop ways in which he could more effectively help his team learn through their interactions with him – and for him to learn through them – at the touchpoint at which they connected.

Domain 2: Igniting connective energy at the touchpoint

Domain 2 focuses on the leader's ability to:

- Affirm the positive qualities of difference in a way that also reinforces the difference – catalysing new insights and connections.

- Open up the possibilities for collective action by igniting connective energy at the touchpoint – valuing friction as a rich source of that energy.

- Catalyse growth and creativity through exchange, trust and mutual learning.

This second domain represents the qualities of the touchpoint itself, requiring a quality of *attention* that both impacts and is impacted by the multiple needs and perspectives present in the moment – the leader's own and those of others. It also relies on a willingness and ability to appreciate and be influenced by the different perspectives and experiences that each person brings to the touchpoint, and to remain alert to the risks of diminution and waste that can occur when the tensions catalysed by difference are smoothed over, ignored or even crushed in an attempt to achieve homogeneity or expediency.

We know that the 'touchpoint' therefore is a moment of interaction between two or more people in a relationship, at which, through the behaviour of any member, in that specific context, there is a sufficient energy[26] that the relationship will be changed – either for better or worse. Conant and Norgaard[27] hold a similar position in their description of a touchpoint being 'spring-loaded' with possibilities – with the power to build or break a relationship, however brief the interaction.

Affirming the positive qualities of difference – catalysing new insights and connections We know that we feel different with different people – some affirm our worth, make us feel energetic and alive, while others drain our vitality and engender in us a negative sense of ourselves as we struggle to feel heard or valued in their company. As Boyatzis and McKee[28] point out, 'We are literally "wired" to pick up subtle clues from one another – and therefore, in a sense, we are dependent on one another for our emotions.' It is natural for us to be attracted to those people who make us feel more energetic, and to spend less time with – even avoid – those who have the reverse effect, especially in our personal lives. The encouragement to the leader in domain 2 is to draw on more of ourselves to unlock positive connection and energy from more relationships than occur naturally, so that he or she can get the best from the diverse resources within the enterprise.

We invite you to reflect for a moment about an interaction that you had recently with someone at work that impacted on your level of energy. What happened in that interaction? How did the other person's actions or behaviour impact on you? What is your sense of how your presence may have impacted on them? Was there a moment when the energy increased? Or decreased? Can you identify how your behaviour or that of the other person contributed to this change in energy? Is there anything you might do differently as a result of this reflection?

With your own experience in mind, we invite you to look more closely at what we are saying happens at this point of interaction – the 'touchpoint' – that shapes our presence in the world, how people see and receive us, and our own sense of self. The following case provides an illustration.

CASE STUDY

Alastair was a CEO of the FMCG business that he had built up himself. He had a lot of respect for his marketing director, Angela, but he occasionally became agitated by her tendency to be reticent in executive meetings. He reacted the same way to two or three other members of his executive team if he felt that they were not fully prepared. In Angela's case, there were moments in meetings when he felt that she was timid about providing the information he needed, and he felt she was not stepping up to her role or doing herself justice. At these times he would pose a question directly to her in the hope of encouraging her to be specific and to open up.

For her part, Angela liked and respected the CEO and generally felt valued by him. However, she often felt on edge in executive meetings in case Alastair 'went for her'. When he posed such a direct question to her, clearly agitated with her, she was triggered into what she felt to be a frightened place. On deep reflection these moments catapulted her back to a time when she was 6 or 7 years old when she was upset at not getting 100 per cent in a spelling test. She felt small, ashamed and timid and she knew that she looked embarrassed and incoherent.

The emotions that arose in Alastair in these 'touchpoint' moments, and the emotional response triggered in Angela, meant that both were not enabling creative use of their abilities or of the potential in their relationship. Therefore their joint value was diminished, not just in one meeting but in the patterns of interactions that followed in subsequent meetings. The same dynamic was present between Alastair and others of his direct reports such that he was not getting the most from their potential contributions as a leadership team.

FIGURE 1.3   Interpersonal dynamic at the touchpoint

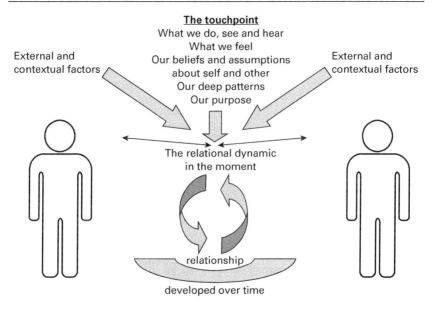

Figure 1.3 illustrates the dynamics of the touchpoint in this story. In the example given here, the moments of interaction in executive meetings, influenced by the assumptions and beliefs that each brought with them, and by the pressures on the business to perform, were leading to a gradual deterioration in the longer-term relationship between these two people, and in the performance of the executive team generally. Angela's personal confidence was decreasing, as was Alastair's confidence in her. It was not until they were each encouraged to see the value of their different styles and to understand how to manage their knee-jerk responses to each other, that they were able to build a productive relationship in which they could get the best from each other.

But while the touchpoint is a moment influenced by multiple factors – as shown in Figure 1.3 – it is also a moment of choice. As Angela started to explore the deep assumptions that she carried about needing to 'have the perfect mark out of 100',[29] she started to see that she could choose to respond differently to what she had seen as Alastair's aggression: she could stay present in meetings and not lose her cool. And as Alastair started to see her increased confidence, he became less inclined to 'encourage' her, and to trust that she would offer the opinion and data that he needed from her.

Opening up possibilities for collective action by igniting connective energy at the touchpoint – valuing friction as a rich source of that energy We see many examples of people in organizations failing to recognize and realize the choices available to them, and potentially giving up the value of difference they bring. It is particularly prevalent in our conversations with high-potential women when, experiencing challenging dynamics in the organizations where they work in the minority, they often tell us that the only way to survive is to 'fit in'. Our challenge to them is to examine a broader range of choices at those touchpoint moments where they feel tempted to fall into submission, and to explore whether there are ways of relating to their male colleagues in a way in which new learning can evolve, which would facilitate teamworking of benefit to both the organization and the woman herself. By remaining alert and open to learning we have the capacity to both strengthen our individual identities and capacities as leaders *and* reinforce our difference – avoiding the risk of 'smoothing over'.[30]

If we look around us, it is easy to spot touchpoint moments where difference leads to destructive friction in the body language that people use, both one-to-one and in larger meetings. In helping two senior leaders develop their relationship it became evident that the more demanding and anxious one leader became with the other, the more the second man leaned back in his chair. The latter's unconscious intent was to deflect the felt aggression coming from his colleague; the impact of this body movement on the other was that he felt more anxious because he thought the other was not taking the issue seriously or showing respect for his views. Only when they were invited to see the dynamic through an objective lens were they able to see how they were missing each other in terms of collaborative contact. The development of self and other awareness enabled them to unlock the suboptimal habitual pattern of their interaction and create new possibilities for their joint leadership.

The vignette in the previous section about the CEO and IT director illustrates how relationships at the top of a business can be allowed to stay unconnected and unresolved through two people lapsing into avoidance. Lencioni[31] similarly observes that the majority of organizations appear to operate at a position in a 'conflict continuum' he labels as 'artificial harmony' – going out of their way to avoid disagreement or challenge that might create discomfort. In Chapter 3 we look at how a temptation to smooth over the different contributions of senior leaders can deny the business critical challenge and objectivity, with potentially dangerous consequences for leadership and governance.

In all these examples, the organization is failing to release the positive energy at the touchpoint that has the potential for creativity and growth. And, as Figure 1.3 shows, the nature of the energy at the touchpoint is not just a result of the people who are in contact – it is highly influenced by the pressures in the outside world. This means that the leader needs also to be able to see the impact of those influences if he or she is to understand the dynamic in the relationship and open up new possibilities for action.

CASE STUDY

An executive team had agreed to take some time out to explore how well they were working as a team. A number of them had realized that they were becoming remote from each other and wanted to explore the reasons and to develop a better way of leading together. Ten minutes after most of the team had gathered, Tom arrived, looking stressed and apparently carrying the tension of the previous meeting on his shoulders. This was a familiar pattern to the rest of the team. As the conversation started to flow it was clear that Tom was still not at ease, until he exploded in frustration at a comment made by another member of the team.

The team sat back and looked at what had happened, and it became clear that this 'vignette' represented the distancing that had developed in the relationship between certain team members. Business performance had been deteriorating for the past three months and Tom was under pressure to provide increasingly detailed revenue and cost data to the Group. This required Tom to ask for more regular updates from the department heads in the team. They had attempted to do this, but some of the team felt unclear about the detail of the requests and also felt dismissed by Tom when they asked questions for clarity. This led them to keep their distance from Tom, an action that led him to see some of them as unhelpful and disinterested in his information and reporting needs. They had become caught in a negative loop and had been unable to see its roots until this moment. Tom brought his frustration from his relationships outside the team, and this dynamic, fed by the demands of the wider organization, had a knock-on effect on his own team's interactions.

It is often easier to see the value of good leadership relationships *after* they have become problematic rather than before. The essence of Touchpoint Leadership is that leaders are alert and responsive to the tensions that can lead to destructive conflict *before* the event and consciously and deliberately help co-create the conditions that encourage energy and coherence from difference. Often teams focus primarily on the 'what' of their task – strategy, objectives and actions – and pay far less attention to the quality of the climate that is needed from their key people and stakeholders for such positive energy to come into being. We introduce case stories in Chapters 4 and 5 where leaders have consciously and proactively set out to work more effectively in relationships – with clients and with teams – to open new possibilities for joint working, business development and enhanced leadership of change.

A fundamental principle of the Gestalt field of psychotherapy is that change most effectively occurs when people – individually or collectively – slow down and become more of what they truly are, through the experience of the present moment. As Clarkson says, 'In this way people can let themselves become totally what they already are, and what they potentially can become. This fullness of experience can be available to them both in the course of their life and in the experience of a single moment.'[32] Developing an awareness of the dynamics of the present moment and the potential of difference within it requires a slowing down, and an expressing of curiosity about what is going on in the space between the players present. Our experience shows us that this slowing down most often leads to faster results, as the leader more fluently learns to spot the start of unproductive interpersonal dynamics before they become destructive. Chapter 5 illustrates the new perspectives and learning that can be stimulated when the participants within an organization actively stand back and look at their relationship in a new light.

This quality of *attention* at the touchpoint is necessarily accompanied by a *willingness* to respect the others in the relationship and be open to new possibilities. Isaacs uses the term 'respecting' to describe the qualities of attention we pay to each other, our social behaviour, our ability to form mutuality, to transform traditional authority relationships into ones of mutual respect; and 'suspending' to denote a willingness to loosen our grip on learnt ways of seeing and thinking and doing, and learning to gain new perspective. With him we see these qualities as integral to cultivating the conditions under which we grow and change in interaction with each other.

Catalysing growth and creativity through exchange, trust and mutual learning We know both from our own work and that of others[33] that it is through interaction with other people that we actually change and develop. In the psychological field, the work on attachment has shown that patterns of connection between parent and child significantly influence the child's development and growth.[34] In addition, the massive advance in recent years in our understanding of the functioning of the brain has enabled us to appreciate some of the physiology behind such a phenomenon. Lewis, Armini and Lannon[35] describe how the part of the brain known as 'limbic' provides us with a capacity to tune into the inner emotional states of others, without the power of logical thought provided by the neo-cortex, a capacity called 'limbic resonance'. They also describe how, through limbic regulation, 'the human body constantly fine-tunes many thousands of physiologic parameters' to other human beings with whom they are closely connected. More recently, Siegel[36] has emphasized the 'open system' nature of the mind and the impact of social interaction in changing the ways the cells of the brain actually grow and work. Building on the growing body of work on the value of mindfulness to health and wellbeing, he argues that 'the way we pay attention in the moment can directly improve the functioning of the body and brain'. Doidge[37] introduces numerous clinical and scientific case studies that show the capacity of the adult brain to transform itself as a result of the way it is used: 'The idea that the brain is like a muscle that grows with exercise is not just a metaphor.'

Our central position in domain 2 is that the leader has the power to enable people to learn together, for the benefit of the enterprise and for themselves, by bringing attention and relational agility to the touchpoint. It is through this specific point of connection between themselves and others that they can catalyse their collective and con-nected learning, and also grow in their own leadership.[38] Throughout this book we show how this individual point of connection or dis-connection has the power to radiate into the wider system. The way in which a leader can attend to the process of broadening the influ-ence of his or her interaction to the wider system is the subject of domain three.

Domain 3: Building and sustaining the collaborative enterprise

Domain 3 of Touchpoint Leadership focuses on developing the capacity to engender a culture of learning and collaboration across the organization, taking a systemic view of the connections that need to be made to build collective value. This draws on the capacity of the leader to both identify where the critical connections need to happen and the conditions that need to be present to both sustain and grow them. As they co-create the collaborative enterprise, we expect touchpoint leaders to:

- Build and facilitate connections across the organization as a critical source of engagement and insight.

- Catalyse connective and sustainable habits of learning that enable the organization to evolve and adapt.

- Co-create a climate of mutual trust that enables individuals to act responsibly and freely.

Building and facilitating connections across the organization – both vertically and horizontally – as a critical source of engagement and insight In addressing the challenges raised by seeking to help leadership teams connect the organization to bring about change we have been drawn increasingly to include in our work the group of managers and leaders who sit at the level just below the executive leadership team. This group has emerged as a critical source of collective power and influence, often caught between the competing expectations and needs of those leading them and those they lead – while also holding the key to collective focus and motivation. We refer to this group as the 'middles', borrowing the terminology from Barry Oshry[39] whose work on systems has identified the likely behavioural patterns of three levels of activity within an organization: the 'tops' representing the executive leadership group, the 'middles' as described here, and the 'bottoms' they lead.

We have found that the middles' capacity to connect – and disconnect – the collective activity of the organization puts them right at the core of the collaborative enterprise. In Chapter 5 we demonstrate how this works in action, sharing the stories of two clients who successfully established the conditions necessary to make it work just at the moment when their organizations most needed it. One of them, a small-scale business aiming to increase its commercial impact, helped create the opportunity for its 'middles' to make an essential contribution to the operational planning process. In the other, a large and complex organization of over 5,000 employees distributed over several geographic locations, the CEO deliberately chose to work with the 100 or more 'middles' as a way of preparing her executive team for their own leadership role.

Standing back from the examples we know that both clients recognized that these 'middle' managers and leaders had an influential role to play in the here and now, helping connect together the disparate threads of their increasingly distributed businesses. They also anticipated that these same people had the potential to become even more significant in the future, forming the new leadership on which business sustainability would depend.

Touchpoint Leadership also draws on the value implicit in making the connections horizontally, and can offer a way of looking at teams that pays attention to both their technical contribution and their broader professional contribution. We use the following example to illustrate this, sharing the story of one client as he sought to increase the impact of his team across the organization as it embarked on yet another phase of the global transformation agenda.

CASE STUDY

Trevor, a finance director, had spent just over a year putting together a team he felt would be able to deliver on the increasingly complex agenda. He was not altogether confident that he had all the capability in place but was ready to move the team on to the next level of operation. As a finance business partner in one of the company's largest operating divisions he was keen to find a way in which he could connect the sometimes conflicting pulls of his business unit role with his role as a leader in the organization's finance community, and wanted to share this with his new team. He held the firm view that they each belonged to two teams – the technical team that supported the business unit, and the broader professional team that provided the overall business with sound financial insights and robust planning. He saw it as a two-tier way of connecting his team to the business and felt that if the team could begin to understand his vision they would step up into the roles he had in mind for them. At the same time he was anxious that they might feel overwhelmed by the possibilities, and that he might be acting prematurely.

As he stood back from this challenge and reflected deeply, it became clear that he needed to *include* his team in the thinking process he was going through. Excluding them meant he was assuming limits to their ability that he had not in fact tested out. He realized that in limiting their participation he was denying himself their different perspectives, and began instead to plan an inquiry day with them. He was clearly uncomfortable at first with the lack of control this approach seemed to represent to him but he was prepared to try it. He knew intuitively that it was only through engendering their engagement with the question, and drawing them in to co-inquire with him, that he would be able to make the changes.

The story illustrates how one client understood the need to extend his team horizontally, and to encourage them to act as members of a larger community of professionals. In this structure power is synonymous with the energy co-created at the touchpoint – which in turn frees up the participants to act both collectively (in Trevor's case as a finance community) and individually (as a finance business partner within a division). Lojeski and Reilly[40] put forward a similar notion in their work on operating within a virtual workforce, suggesting that rather than teams we consider a much lighter way of holding individuals together across boundaries, as a vibrant community in which touchpoints and the relationships that help form them are central to organizational effectiveness. They refer to them as 'virtual ensembles'.

This story also demonstrates how an individual leader can cause his own limitation by not acting in a connected way – in this case, assuming that he must first resolve the question and only then invite others to join him in its implementation. Connection and collaboration across boundaries depends on the ability to open up the space and create a quality of relationship or touchpoint that is defined more by its capacity to 'pull' than its capacity to 'push'. This concept of 'pull' is fundamental to Touchpoint Leadership and is built on the underlying ability of individuals and teams to connect dialogically, curiously and affirmatively. Hagel, Seely Brown and Davison[41] offer the concept of 'pull' as a powerful way of understanding and working with the need to attract people in such a way that we increase our collective understanding and effectiveness and turn uncertainty into opportunity – the smallest of moves able to achieve outsized impact – and in Chapter 5 we share more examples of where this capacity for making generative connections has made a significant contribution to business effectiveness.

Engendering connective and sustainable habits of learning that enable the organization to evolve and adapt Learning at the touchpoint depends on maintaining a capacity to be curious, to experience the connective links across boundaries as opportunities to maximize their inherent difference, and above all to remain aware of the impact these different perspectives and value systems may have on the meaning that emerges. It is therefore critical that leaders enable their teams to cascade a climate of learning that encourages creative connections beyond the boundaries of their own teams, reaching out beyond the boundaries to engage in learning conversations with those who also sit at the edge of their businesses. We see how significant this can be in Chapter 4, when we focus on the impact of Touchpoint Leadership in professional services firms where the connection itself helps generate the 'living brand'.

As the relational connections multiply across the organization it is essential that leaders can hold open the channels that enable their collective insights to flow, ensuring the organization both draws on the learning and integrates it into its operational sense-making. Linda Gratton[42] goes some way towards describing the conditions necessary to make this happen with her notion of the 'hot spot', describing it as a source of energy that is built from a combination of a cooperative mindset, the capacity to span organizational boundaries (the broader the span the greater the innovation) and a vision or collective task that together ignite at the point of connection to form an energy that in turn becomes translated into outcomes by the productive capacity of the people in the system.

Working with individual clients to become both self-aware and self-correcting we have been increasingly convinced that these leaders can also help create organizations that are able to learn and evolve, engendering a capacity to innovate, maximize differences and draw in the support and energy needed to achieve their business outcomes. One client began to explore his organization's capacity to connect in this way when he asked us to support him in creating a capacity for learning that would help his people withstand the demotivating challenges of continual organizational restructuring. He held a clear vision that *connective* learning – that is, learning that would help join the insights and activities of his people – would create a level of resilience that would be critical to maintaining focus and momentum in the next phase of the transformation programme. As we worked with him and his leadership team to explore how they could make it happen, it became clear that they would first have to let go of a reliance on the stability of the organizational structure and instead rely on the strength of their relationships and their ability to sustain focus together[43] to provide effective leadership to the business.

We stress that the learning must be *connective*, and in some of the client stories in later chapters illustrate how organizations themselves can inadvertently encourage the very blockers that inhibit these connections. We also share the story of one client who was able to use a focus on connective learning to surmount the challenges of an organizational structure that clearly conflicted with his team's ability to work effectively together. In all cases the ability to pay attention to the quality of their relationships and touchpoints, and the potential impact of the system within which they were operating, was key to their success.

Co-creating a climate of mutual trust that enables individuals to act responsibly and freely Working in domain 3 has caused us to stand back and consider how trust can so easily break down – between colleagues, between levels in an organization, between an organization and its customers or clients. We have witnessed it first-hand alongside our clients and have observed the impact when the loss of trust becomes systemic and global. As new governance and control have been applied in the aftermath of each crisis we have joined those who welcomed its reassurances – yet at the same time have also become concerned at the potential polarization it can cause towards a form of leadership that seeks to restrict and mitigate risk rather than optimize the courage and vision that carries promises of innovation and growth.

As we look to the future we are increasingly certain that touchpoint leaders will need to be able to address these challenges, building sufficient confidence in their colleagues, teams and organizations so that they are able to trust them to operate freely. In Chapter 2 we invite you to pause and reflect on your own leadership, and explore the stories of others who have similarly given this quality of attention to their own leadership. Some questions to help frame deeper reflection are included in Chapter 6.

Notes

1 Bradford, D I and Cohen, A R identified the negative impact of the 'heroic leader' on performance in *Managing for Excellence* (Hoboken, NJ, Wiley, 1984).

2 In *Power Up: Transforming organizations through shared leadership* (Hoboken, NJ, Wiley, 1998) they offer the description of post-heroic leadership which is later developed by Joiner and Josephs, detailed in note 3.

3 Joiner and Josephs respond to the global challenges of accelerating change and growing complexity and interdependence with a leadership development framework built on the qualities of leadership agility – described by them as representing the capacity 'to take wise and effective action amid complex, rapidly changing conditions... an intentional, proactive stance' in *Leadership Agility: Five levels of mastery for anticipating and initiating change* (San Francisco, Jossey Bass, 2007).

4 Goleman, D (1998) *Working with Emotional Intelligence* (London, Bloomsbury).

5 Carr, N (2010) *The Shallows: How the internet is changing the way we think, read and remember* (Atlantic Books).

6 Boyatzis, R and McKee, A (2005) *Resonant Leadership* (Boston, MA, Harvard Business School Press).

7 Ibarra, H and Hansen, M T (2011) 'Are you a collaborative leader?', *Harvard Business Review,* July-August 2011. The authors state: 'The ability to bring together people from different backgrounds, disciplines, cultures and generations and leverage all they have to offer, therefore, is a must-have for leaders. Yet many companies spend inordinate amounts of time, money and energy attracting talented employees only to subject them to homogenizing processes that kill creativity.'

8 CIPD Report, March 2012, *Where has all the trust gone?*

9 Kleiner, A and Rutger von Post (2001) 'A corporate climate of mutual help', *Strategy and Business*, 62, Spring. In an interview with the authors, Schein says, 'Better teamwork requires perpetual mutual helping, within and across hierarchical boundaries', and later: 'In any

helping situation, "humble inquiry" is a key intervention to equilibrate the relationship between the vulnerable person asking for help and the powerful helper.' See also Schein, E H (2011) *Helping: How to offer, give and receive help* (San Francisco, Berrett-Koehler).

10 Oshry, B (2007) *Seeing Systems: Unlocking the mysteries of organizational life* (San Francisco, Berrett-Koehler). In his work on organizational systems, Barry Oshry shows how systems habitually generate conflict at points of difference (what he calls 'door A' responses). He also argues that people need to develop awareness of self and systemic patterns to enable points of difference to enable partnership ('door B' responses).

11 A development programme founded on the principles of self-awareness and mindfulness has been running since 2007. This programme, developed and led by Chade-Meng Tan, and built on Daniel Goleman's work on emotional intelligence and Jon Kabat-Zinn's teachings on mindfulness, is described in detail in Tan, Chade-Meng (2012) *Search Inside Yourself* (London, Collins).

12 Lee, G (2005) *Leadership Coaching: From personal insight to organizational performance* (London, CIPD). Graham Lee points out that it is not enough for the leader to explore his (sic) own 'authentic self': he must connect his personal convictions in a way that is 'attuned to the organization', creating an authentic leadership style that arises from the paradox of personal versus organizational goals.

13 Kegan, R and Lahey, L L (2009) *Immunity to Change: How to overcome it and unlock the potential in yourself and your organization* (Boston, MA, Harvard Business School Press).

14 Marshall, J (1984) *Women Managers: Travellers in a male world* (Chichester, Wiley) warns of a dysfunctional 'communion strategy' in her work on women managers where she describes a propensity to consider it easier to accept or go along with a stereotyped role rather than resist it. This can become a form of self-distortion and suppression.

15 Rowan, J (2001) The humanistic approach to action research, in P Reason and H Bradbury (eds) *Handbook of Action Research: Participatory inquiry & practice* (London, Sage).

16 George, B (2007) *True North: Discover your authentic leadership* (San Francisco, Jossey-Bass).

17 Boyatzis, R and McKee, A (2005) *Resonant Leadership* (Boston MA, Harvard Business School Press).

18 Schon, D A (1991) *The Reflective Practitioner* (Aldershot, Ashgate) describes reflection-in-action as a 'reflective conversation with the situation' and demonstrates how practitioners can draw on elements of their familiar repertoire, reframe a problem or evolve a new and generative metaphor to propel their knowing forward. He presents it very much as a process of self-awareness.

19 Rosenwald and Ochberg pose this question: 'Can a person by telling her (sic) story rescue her understanding from both accidental and formal self-misunderstanding and inadvertent self-misrepresentation? Can life stories be opened up, as well as cramped, in the telling?' in their book *Storied Lives: The cultural politics of self-understanding* (New Haven CT, Yale University Press, 1992).

20 Gratton, L (2004) *The Democratic Enterprise: Liberating your business with freedom, flexibility and commitment* (London, Prentice Hall/FT). In describing how individuals become autonomous in the democratic enterprise she talks of individuals reframing themselves as investors rather than as assets, and the necessary commitment to a 'reflective, conscious process of self-development and learning'.

21 In her PhD thesis 'From the inside out', Jacqui Scholes-Rhodes develops a combined practice of dialogue and inquiry and presents it as 'a creative art of inquiry' (PhD thesis 2002, University of Bath, http://www.actionresearch.net/living/rhodes.shtml).

22 Isaacs, W (1999) *Dialogue and the Art of Thinking Together* (New York, Currency Doubleday).

23 Bohm, D (1996) *On Dialogue* (London, Routledge).

24 Goleman, D (2006) *Social Intelligence: The new science of human relationships* (London, Bantam). Goleman builds on his earlier work on emotional intelligence by identifying two key elements of social intelligence – social awareness, comprising primal empathy, attunement, empathic accuracy and social cognition; and social facility, comprising synchrony, self-presentation, influence and concern.

25 Goleman, D, ibid, note 4.

26 Bruch, H and Vogel, B (2011) *Fully Charged: How great leaders boost their organization's energy and ignite high performance* (Boston MA, Harvard Business Review Press). They build an energy matrix that illustrates four states of organizational energy – the goal being 'productive energy'.

27 Conant, D and Norgaard, M (2011) *Touchpoints: Creating powerful leadership connections in the smallest of moments* (San Francisco, Jossey-Bass). They describe the touchpoint as being spring-loaded with possibilities – with the power to build or break a relationship, however brief the interaction. They consider three aspects or 'variables' that come together to create a touchpoint: the leader, the issue and the other people. They also refer to the exponential effect Touchpoint Leadership can have by transmitting through human networks. By developing touchpoint mastery they track how a leader can transform an ordinary interaction into an extraordinary one. Their structured approach to developing mastery attends to how leaders think and make sense of the world, the code by which they live and therefore engage authentically, and the competence and readiness to act as a touchpoint leader (head, heart and hands). They assume the capacity to be fully present and to build meaningful relationships. Their proposition is also very much aligned to the model of 'servant leadership'.

28 Ibid, note 17.

29 The idea that we carry with us stories about ourselves or 'scripts' derived from early life experiences is core to transactional analysis, a field of psychotherapy. See Stewart, I and Joines, V (1987) *Introduction to TA* (Lifespace) and Steiner, C (1974) *Scripts People Live* (Grove Press).

30 Marshall, J (1984) *Women Managers: Travellers in a male world* (Chichester: Wiley) warns of a dysfunctional 'communion strategy' in her work on women managers where she describes a propensity to consider it easier to accept or go along with a stereotyped role rather than resist it. This can become a form of self-distortion and suppression.

31 Lencioni, P (2012) *The Advantage: Why organizational health trumps everything else in business* (San Francisco, Jossey-Bass) puts forward the concept of the 'conflict continuum', on which he maps the 'ideal conflict point'. He observes that the majority of organizations appear to operate at the extreme he labels as 'artificial harmony' – going out of their way to avoid disagreement or challenge that might create discomfort. He proposes that the healthiest place is just off-centre, moving slightly away from the ideal conflict point to ensure we remain engaged in all the constructive conflict we can have, but never stepping over the line into destructive territory. Moving to this place – and operating effectively from there – depends on being prepared to be vulnerable and on building courage and trust.

32 Clarkson, P (2004) *Gestalt Counselling in Action*, 3rd edn (London, Sage).

33 Kegan, R (1982) *The Evolving Self: Problem and process in human development* (Cambridge MA, Harvard University Press) develops a framework that defines five stages of determining self and its relationship to others and the wider whole of community. Stage five of the model is 'interindividual balance', described as an ability to co-mingle in such a way that distinct identities are guaranteed.

34 Bowlby, J (1988) *A Secure Base: Clinical applications of attachment theory* (London, Routledge).

35 Lewis, T, Armini, F and Lannon, R (2001) *A General Theory of Love* (London, Vintage).

36 Siegel, D J (2007) *The Mindful Brain* (New York, Norton).

37 Doidge, N (2008) *The Brain that Changes Itself* (London, Penguin).

38 Senge, P M (1990) *The Fifth Discipline: The art and practice of the learning organization* (New York, Century Business).

39 Oshry, B (2007) *Seeing Systems: Unlocking the mysteries of organizational life* (San Francisco, Berrett-Koehler).

40 Lojeski, K S and Reilly, R R (2008) *Uniting the Virtual Workforce: Transforming leadership and innovation in the globally integrated enterprise* (Hoboken NJ, Wiley & Sons). Their research and consulting in diverse organizations has led them to the conclusion that improving the effectiveness of the virtual workforce does not lie in better technology. They have coined the phrase 'virtual distance' to describe a feeling of being psychologically distant – taking into account both real distance and perceived spaces that can arise for numerous reasons – and measure three factors: physical distance, operational distance and affinity distance. 'Affinity distance' is when we don't establish the kinds of personal relationships that satisfy our social needs. When this is high, 'a powerful psychological wall bars effective collaboration'. They focus on the significance of cultural, social, relationship and interdependence distance. They also draw correlations with 'cognitive trust' and 'affective trust'. They refer to a 'new' leader as 'ambassadorial... a boundary spanner'.

41 Hagel, J, Seely Brown, J and Davison, L (2010) *The Power of Pull: How small moves, smartly made, can set big things in motion* (New York, Basic Books).

42 Gratton, L (2007) develops a similar argument about the creative power of connecting across difference in *Hot Spots: Why some companies buzz with energy and innovation – and others don't* (London, Prentice Hall/FT). She offers the notion of the 'hot spot' as a source of energy that is built from a combination of a cooperative mindset (quality of relationships is crucial to forming this), the capacity to span organizational boundaries (the broader the span the greater the innovation) and a vision or collective task that together ignite at the point of connection to form an energy that in turn becomes translated into outcomes by the productivity capacity of people in the system. The outcome is innovation and value creation. It is critical that the people can work productively together, engage in reflexive conversations, resolve conflict together and have the networks to support them.

43 Ibid, note 41; Hagel *et al* refer to 'creation spaces' as a means of attracting performance-driven teams to foster rich interactions both within and across other teams and need to pay attention to three critical components: the participants, the interactions they might develop and the environment that would be necessary to make them work.

Priming the touchpoint to become relational

02

When leaders do their best work they draw on their own fundamental values and capabilities – operating in a frame of mind that is true to them yet, paradoxically, not their normal state of being. (MOMENTS OF GREATNESS. ENTERING THE FUNDAMENTAL STATE OF LEADERSHIP, ROBERT E QUINN, *HBR*, JULY–AUG 2005, THE HIGH-PERFORMANCE ORGANIZATION)

In Chapter 1 we introduced the notion of Touchpoint Leadership as the capacity to ignite and align energy, action and passion across the organization by focusing on the need to connect. We referred to working towards a 'three-tiered connectivity', helping individuals connect with themselves, with their teams and groups, and across the organization and its stakeholders. In Chapters 2 to 5 we demonstrate how we build on this framework, all the time working with the paradoxical assumptions that sit at the heart of this form of leadership as we help leaders work at the touchpoint to *connect* rather than integrate the polarities that might otherwise signify difference and diversity.

In this chapter we focus on *priming* the touchpoint, working with individual leaders to pause and consider how they might bring themselves to the point of connection with others, enabling the conditions necessary to help co-create value at the touchpoints across the business. We track how a number of leaders have explored the values, behaviours, beliefs and motivations that have helped form and re-form their leadership, and demonstrate how this focus has helped strengthen their ability to lead with a relational perspective. We put the focus on awareness of self and of others as a critical leadership capability, building on the business's need for leaders who can help connect individual passion and values, and in this way generate the collective energy that will help deliver sustainable business success.

We know from our client work that as leaders stand back from their day-to-day role some may come to see that their leadership has been compromised, lacking the deep values and intent that initially gave them energy. It is from this realization that they begin to understand that both they and their business will be best served by their ability to bring more of themselves into play at work, embodying their values and purpose in a way that is so much bigger than the fractionated 'self' who habitually turns up as leader. They appreciate what it takes to bring in their individual difference in a way that has impact and influence, and make enormous investment in their personal development to ensure they fully understand how to achieve it. We are therefore proposing that leaders need to develop and draw on three interrelated capacities to be successful touchpoint leaders, each aspect catalytic in enabling the other.

Being fully present at the touchpoint

This is the leaders' capacity to be fully aware of their 'whole' self and knowing how they manifest it in their leadership role. It requires leaders to be aware of their own deeply held values and how they impact the way in which they lead and bring meaning to their role. It also demands an acute appreciation of how their deep-seated beliefs may help shape connections with others and either help or hinder the touchpoint as a source of relational energy. And it requires leaders to hold themselves morally accountable to these principles, both within the organization and on its boundaries.

Personal growth through interaction at the touchpoint

This second capacity defines the curiosity, humility and perseverance that keep leaders permanently at their learning edge – helping challenge today's 'truth' about themselves and others and encouraging innovation and improvisation as they connect with others. It challenges the leader to see touchpoints as a potential source of personal growth and liberation, and as a means of becoming 'whole'. In this capacity a leader must have the courage to hold on to the tension and friction at the touchpoint, to avoid the temptation to smooth over, avoid or even crush the difference from which new learning and growth can evolve.

Developing a relational perspective

This third 'priming' capacity requires leaders to see themselves through a relational lens, willing to explore and develop their ways of relating to generate optimum value for the business. It invites leaders to be constantly open and attentive to the qualities of exchange and reciprocity as a source of power and influence, growing an awareness of the power of leadership that lies in the space between people. Relationships conduct the force that enables these exchanges to be made, and require leaders to be able to adapt their ways of connecting with others to engender active engagement at the touchpoint.

We explore each of these three capacities in turn, drawing on our work with leaders from a range of sectors and organizations. We offer insights from their explorations as they seek to understand themselves fully from the inside out, exploring their connectedness at an intra-personal level and finding ways to release the energy of their individual purpose and values. We illustrate how in some cases the individuals were not yet able to make the step, the impact of the system within which they found themselves living and working too strong at that time for them to realize their full potential. As we do this we offer questions that we hope will encourage you to reflect on your own leadership, a process of self-development that we return to in Chapter 6.

Being fully present at the touchpoint

Developing connected leadership: the power of sharing personal stories

We start with a story that shows the connecting power that can be released within a leadership team when they each take time to reflect on and share what deeply matters to them.

CASE STUDY

We had been asked to work with a senior leadership team to help them find ways of working effectively together so that they could lead a significant transformation programme across the company. After spending the first hour or so getting to know them we had a very clear sense of their intellectual commitment to the task but felt very little emotional connection in the room. They were barely present and seemed to be struggling to find ways of connecting.

We knew that if we focused on their team processes before addressing this lack of emotional connection there was a strong risk that any implementation of actions would be half-hearted. We needed to address this before we could move on to action and therefore asked them to consider three things:

1   The most important influence in their life.

2   Their most memorable event or moment.

3   One dream they'd like to fulfil.

Each had a flipchart and coloured pens – and the instruction that they could use only pictures. Half an hour later they were so busy drawing that they didn't hear us ask if they'd finished. Finally we asked them to stop and, as we had a huge gallery space at the end of the room, invited them to put their posters up there. One by one they shared their stories, powerful stories that entirely changed the atmosphere in the room. Although we've done a similar exercise many times before we'd never had this sort of result. We do need to respect their confidentiality and the trust they displayed in us but we can say that each one of them shared a deeply emotional story. It was clear from their reactions that they had not known anything about their shared experiences beforehand, and that in the moment of sharing something had shifted significantly for them – a level of openness, trust, some personal disclosure. It was also clear that the team had begun to form a very different quality of connection. The touchpoint had become live for them.

As they continued to share their stories another common thread emerged from their collective dreams that was also significant. Each one represented an aspiration to stretch their boundaries, to travel, to sail, to fly – and there was such a sense of liberation in the room that it flowed into a conversation about how they had all felt so tied up by the last six months of constant drive and personal pressure. Again, it was an outcome we could not have predicted – but in that moment of sharing each had primed the touchpoint to such an extent that they were able to form a connection that subsequently sustained them through 18 months of instability and change in the business.

This story helps illustrate our belief that leaders need to be fully present before they can realize their full impact. They need to be clear in their purpose and to recognize how they constantly draw meaning from a deep appreciation of the values that help form and re-form that purpose. These values are shaped by a capacity to care and be emotionally honest, and we encourage leaders to hold themselves to account by knowing acutely how this impacts the moral compass that shapes their thinking and action. This is how we understand personal governance in a world that demands that leaders learn to have less control through distributed and networked organizational structures – often spread across global boundaries – while at the same time taking a greater accountability for the outcomes. This is about being on purpose for the collective good.

We saw the importance of this in another organization where a team of highly expert leaders had been tasked with creating a community of practice within a matrix organization. For months this team had been grappling with how to create enough leadership presence to have influence across the performance-driven business. It was not until they took time out to think about what mattered deeply to each one of them personally that a sense of energizing purpose emerged among the team, generating a desire to get out and talk about it with their community.

This ability of leaders to connect with their inner selves – the values that motivate them, give meaning and purpose, and by which they will assess the impact of their ultimate legacy – inevitably defines their difference and it's the capacity to realize this difference that we observe as critical to the formation of the touchpoint. It does mean holding a quality of tension at the touchpoint, and it will be necessary to recognize when the point of difference is just too great for connection. At that point we encourage leaders to ask themselves questions such as: How can I acknowledge my difference and hold the tension side by side with our collective identity? How can I appreciate my own difference first then find ways to connect with others that both respects and helps realize the value of *our* difference?

As we mention in Chapter 1, there has been much written about authentic leadership and many leaders have achieved tremendous success through exploring their own journeys on the path to defining the 'true' them. At the same time we encourage them to consider that this sense of being is dynamic, changing as they absorb the experiences of each touchpoint and as they seek to find useful coherence in the complexity. We also encourage them to distinguish between 'what I know now' and 'what I might know at a future point'. This ability to 'know' cannot be permanent as our insights change so rapidly and we have so little control over external factors – but our capacity to question and learn can be permanent, founded on deep insights into what matters to us personally and which engenders the motivation and passion to lead.

There are some simple questions we put to the leaders who work with us:

- What do you care most about, what matters?
- What sense of purpose do you bring to your work and your leadership?
- What governs your moral compass?
- What makes you want to lead – and what makes you not want to lead anymore?
- What legacy do you want to leave and how does this influence your decisions and actions?

Much of our work has started out with an individual's need to develop a deeper self-awareness, often linked to a need to explore what happens when he or she connects with others. This can be his or her connections as a leader, a colleague, a partner – and can include working both inside and outside the boundary of the organization.

This work has increasingly shown that many leaders are conflicted in their role, and the challenges are growing. Many come to realize that there is a conflict between their external leadership persona and who they truly are; between their organizational role and their role as parent, family member and friend; between their inherent talent and their ability to apply that talent in a resonant way in their organization; between their personal values and those of the organization. Many struggle in their roles as leaders to reconcile competing values and needs, such as the need for freedom and control or the need for efficiency and innovation.

In some cases we have worked with leaders who assumed that it is necessary to separate 'leader self' from 'whole self' and this in itself has created a disconnect. Sometimes leaders have learnt to bring only part of themselves to work, perhaps because they feel that to be professional they need to contain large parts of their overall personality in order to focus on the 'task'; perhaps because they want to protect their personal life from the intrusion of work. But our experience shows that the long-term consequence for many such leaders is that their work starts to lack personal satisfaction and reward, and their ability to lead becomes limited through their partial engagement. This is not healthy or productive – for the individuals, their family or the organizations they lead.

Working with constructive tension to gain deeper personal insights

If we look deeply we can see that these disconnections often manifest themselves as a battle between personal values and the implicit values of the collective. Dr Jack Whitehead,[1] through his many years of research into the development of leadership in education, refers to this form of tension as a 'living contradiction', his use of the word 'living' an encouragement to consider how deep the tension may go into the personal choices we are making – and to encourage us to appreciate the tension of the contradiction as an essential part of our living. Full awareness of these choices is critical to our emotional health and wellbeing.[2]

In conversation with one leader we asked how important it was that an executive team view difference as an opportunity to learn, and whether they should be prepared to treat the potential tension as healthy and useful. He suggested that an over-emphasis on being close-knit, with its inferences of integration and smoothing-over the sharp edges of difference, could in fact block the opportunity to develop the insights that would otherwise be valuable to the business. He described how in one organization he had observed how difficult it became to introduce new blood into the leadership space once the leadership team itself restricted its own readiness to learn. This is a theme we will develop further in Chapter 5 when we look at the way in which whole groups can become drawn into taking on a buffer role, but it's worth noting here that there are risks in the driving need to smooth over and create homogeneity in the leadership team – and possibly right across the organization – stifling the very difference that catalyses innovation and change.

The same leader went on to talk about the emotional qualities needed in assessing the 'fit' of new people joining the leadership team. He put a great deal of emphasis on the need for empathy, defining empathy as not necessarily agreeing but making the effort to understand, having the capacity to listen, to being aware of the other. In his words:

> *I've seen people with low empathy and that has jarred. I've seen it happen when all the other indicators have signalled that they'll be a good hire and the CEO has disregarded the measures of self and other awareness believing that they'll teach the dog new tricks – we end up either getting rid of them or decide long-term you'll manage around their problems and look for more resilient people to work alongside them.*

In this way the individual becomes a 'difficult person' rather than a participant in a difficult relationship and they eventually find themselves isolated and disempowered. We asked him how he might encourage leaders to develop these insights; he said:

> *We can measure self and other awareness, but often it's a 360-degree review that will highlight the issues. The evidence can emerge very quickly, particularly when we have new members join the team. It's often in the first few weeks that we hear their plan but neither we nor they make an effort to listen or explore – and we're both reluctant to make any adjustments. This is compounded when we bring someone in from a directly comparable business. It may seem that they're exactly the same but there can be huge tissue rejection.*

This sort of 'tissue rejection' can also happen when substantial change happens in the business. The impact is particularly noticeable when the change is catalysed by merger and/or acquisition, and efforts to integrate the old and the new are unable to offer those affected the space in which to explore new connections and relevance. Individuals who were otherwise emotionally engaged and successful in their roles find themselves on the outside looking in, all the connective points that previously held them together somehow fragmented in the change.

Robert became a victim in this way, losing his capacity to connect as he became swallowed up by the forces of a large-scale acquisition. He was unable to let go of the certainties that had previously helped him make sense of role and when we met him had retreated into an un-resourceful place.

CASE STUDY

Operating in the post-acquisition phase of a culturally challenging amalgamation of two European entities, Robert appeared to have very little emotional expression for most of our conversation – except for the moment when he suddenly smiled and shared the delight of remembering the emotional connection he felt with his previous company. When we shared our observation of the physical transformation we had seen – and how the touchpoint had felt to us – we immediately saw its rapid masking. He assured us that he did not intend worrying about emotional connectivity with this new firm.

His lack of emotional presence continued to impact our meetings with him, highlighted only by rare glimpses behind the mask. He held on tight and made it clear that he did not want to embark on a personal exploration; he was neither curious nor prepared to be.

In our first meeting with him we contracted for action planning on his communication style, and in the second he was much more specific in wanting to develop a strategy for dealing with his new boss. He was clear that he only wanted the strategy, and had no intention of changing his behaviours. He resisted any attempt to shine a light on his reluctance to change his behaviour, choosing instead to accept his disconnection. It was clear from peer feedback that this lack of connective presence was having a negative impact on the contribution he was making but he refused to start the journey. He chose instead to remain in a place that was increasingly marked by its lack of meaning and emotional depth.

We include this story as an illustration of the potential damage that can be caused when companies fail to pay attention to the need for connective energy. We have witnessed many such situations where, despite active consultation about how the post-merger business can derive the 'best of both' from the legacy organizations at a practical and tactical level, the deeper beliefs about such things as freedom and/or control, collegiality and/or authority, are left untouched. This can result in individuals, teams and even large-scale groups losing their sense of meaning and shared purpose. The resulting emotional disengagement creates such toxicity in the system that the touchpoints become damaged.

Another client has talked to us about the need to establish one's personal resilience, a kind of toughness that reassures the business that they're not going to crumble under the spotlight of challenge. It's an interesting position, and could imply that we want our leaders to hold their position come what may. It could also imply that we might see those leaders who listen thoughtfully and openly and then subsequently alter their plans as somewhat weaker or less decisive. But this is when the touchpoint is most at risk – the logic of argument simply causing an entrenchment of the different positions and destroying any possibility of a dialogic interchange which might otherwise be generative.

Developing the courage to be different

We recognize that the world needs 'new' strong leaders, leaders who have the courage to be their different selves and have the art of connecting with 'what is' in ways that are effective, generative and catalytic. We need these new contributions to feed strategies that will help re-form business and the organizations that enable them. We are not looking for a capacity to 'fit the mould'. This is not about squeezing new identities into the boardroom in ways that sustain the homogeneous nature of the group, or creating bridges between cultural extremes to absorb the shock of tension. This is about learning to 'be' different – in ways that enrich and affirm and enable full exchange, and that takes courage and curiosity and a readiness to step into unknowing and working through the potential disconnects that may well happen on the way.

CASE STUDY

A 'new generation' leader was working with us on his integration into the UK office of the global firm after several years based in the United States. Anecdotal feedback was suggesting that he didn't 'fit', that he was too driven, too ready to express his view. When given the feedback he replied, 'If I am pacey and driven as an individual, and that is a product of my personal story, then I am being authentic ... and so why does the organization reject me?' Rather than take on the work on a co-inquiry based on his fitting in we suggested a more useful question might be, 'How can I bring my difference into this part of the organization in a way that will catalyse challenge and creativity so that it serves the collective endeavour?' By working with this self-inquiry he was more likely to find a way in which he could maintain authenticity whilst also retelling the story in a way that might serve him better, and also find ways to connect and become whole through that connection. Our focus was therefore on working with him to appreciate what and how he could contribute at the touchpoint, and how he might become whole through that connection.

We know of other examples where high-potential leaders have been rejected by the very organizations that have deliberately set out to attract them for their difference. Neither the individual nor the organization has known how to create the touchpoint in a way that has fed their respective differences, and instead they have experienced a very severe case of tissue-rejection. In other cases we have found that the interest in being authentic and connecting with personal motivation and values has in fact distorted the individual's ability to connect with the collective intent, and we have been brought in to help develop a quality of attention at the macro level as a powerful counterpoint to the drive of individual ambition.

This was played out in one client organization where a new CEO had been appointed to lead the business through an enormous transformation. He had been deliberately recruited for his different background, which he quickly reinforced by recruiting a group of high-potential managers with similar track records. It was a model that had great potential to succeed. But the CEO failed to engage his team of executives in his personal ambition for the business, and they in turn unknowingly blocked the ability of the managers below them to take the lead. Energy was depleted at each touchpoint in the system, with each group of leaders becoming increasingly frustrated at the lack of progress.

The theme is the same: without being able to release the creative energy at the touchpoint leaders are unlikely to fully realize the enormous potential that lies in the difference. The following story illustrates this point.

CASE STUDY

Celia was a 'new' leader struggling to bring in her difference. She was unaware that she was isolating herself – sitting in a 'learnt' position of tough independence that had become non-relational and distorted by ongoing stress in her personal life. This was having a knock-on effect on the friction she was setting up in relationships that were key to her success. Her vulnerability was evident but she did not have the curiosity that would enable her to self-inquire, or at least not to start with. She seemed to put all her energy into defending, protecting her 'self' and needed to be able to trust before exploring the new options.

It was also important at the beginning that we did not automatically assume her MD's perspective that she was a 'difficult person'. It was much more useful to examine how she might be affecting the touchpoints in a way that was experienced as difficult – and to help her develop her ability to recognize and optimize the collective tension she was capable of generating.

Along the way she explored what it meant to have compassion, to extend forgiveness (her old stories), and to accept that none of us is whole or perfect. The turning point for her was the change in her fundamental belief that she needed to cope on her own. Instead she now articulates her most useful belief as 'I can ask people for help' and has developed a greater resonance and alignment between her aspired leadership self and the reality that others experience. Her MD recently described her as 'a joy to work with... a transformation' and has made his trust in her transparent by offering her the opportunity to head up a new entrepreneurial business.

It's important to stress that in developing heightened self-awareness we are not condoning self-centredness. Rather we are encouraging a capacity to develop both self and *other* awareness, often through the telling and sharing of personal stories that help an individual stand back from his or her experiences and begin to see new meaning in them.[3] It's this *other* awareness that provides another critical quality in co-creating the touchpoint and which we develop in the next part of this chapter. This is the point at which we explore how we become whole through our connections, and develop the capacities of exchange and reciprocity as a source of power and influence.

This sense of self can also be impacted by identifying strongly with a specific group or community, the need for collective strength and reassurance sometimes weakening the ability to develop individually. By way of illustration, we worked with a group of women who were exploring how to 'deal with' systemic aggression in their organization and which they experienced as disempowering and energy-sapping. They were experiencing the challenges of trying to succeed in a culture where they were seen as a minority and where they saw the values of the dominant culture as contrary to their own. They talked specifically about the challenges of trying to promote themselves in this context. We asked them what they might liberate if they re-framed 'promoting themselves' as 'generating new touchpoint qualities' from a sense of their own individual difference, and offered these questions to support their inquiry:

- How can you bring in your difference in ways that are inclusive and invitational?
- How can you enable others to feel safe and valued without compromising your own values?
- How can you affirm yourself in a way that contributes to mutual success?
- How can you enable a shift towards mutual learning that will benefit the business?

Values that create anchors for action

Touchpoint Leadership depends on individual leaders being able to explore the connection with their fundamental values, identifying their motivation and energy for the work *and* engaging with their positive and affirmative experiences in such a way that they are able to embody them as connective qualities at the touchpoint. In the examples above we have described cases in which we have worked with leaders who have become detached. Sometimes they have become aware of it themselves – and have been keen to explore and answer the question: 'How can I integrate all parts of my life so that there's purpose in what I individually contribute?' In other cases the degree of detachment has been apparent in their ways of communicating – through words, body and behaviour – and we have been led to ask, 'What is missing that would make you feel whole?' Both these types of situation give rise to new choices about how leaders are living their life, choices that impact not only their own emotional health and wellbeing but, more important, have a significant impact on those with whom they connect.

We have been increasingly conscious of leaders seeking to re-connect in this way as a result of the systemic loss of confidence that has occurred in the financial sector in recent years. As we have seen organizations struggle to deal with criticism from stakeholders, from government, from customers and even from their own people, we have worked with the impact this has had on individuals who aspire to lead the sector to recovery. In some cases they have responded with an expression of high humility and apology which, in turn, has had a negative ricochet effect on morale and levels of confidence within the business. One particular leader experienced the impact of the crisis as a sense of disconnection from himself. He reported losing his passionate presence, experienced by others as a lack of gravitas, and was no longer certain that he had the energy to continue. He was aware of a personal pattern of stepping out, physically withdrawing to gain distance, and disconnecting both emotionally and intellectually every time he came up against resistance. He had reached a point where he was losing his ability to connect with his colleagues, his team and, more important, the role he had to play in the organization's recovery. While this situation could have raised questions about this leader's personal resilience, a much more valuable intervention needed to begin with exploring how a person in this position can reconnect with his or her sense of passion and commitment and change his or her *quality of connection* with the business. By working with the question: 'How can I connect with my own positive energy and ensure that it continues to flow even when the system threatens to disable me?' we can work with a leader or a group of leaders to help arrest the debilitating effects of both the personal and systemic context and through a focus on the touchpoint help build personal and collective confidence that is founded on a clear sense of self and the values that underpin that identity.

Using this approach we have seen individual leaders actively recon-nect with their sense of purpose and explore how they can use that purpose to connect with others, rather than allow it to be squashed or hidden away. We often meet leaders aiming to protect their personal and family life from the stresses at work, drawing a strong line between family self and professional self, and while the strategy can help feed leaders' duty of protection and help them feel in control, in the short term it can also rob them of the energy and resourcefulness they need to be fully present in the business. One leader was able to reconnect with her passion to be a change catalyst in the organization – and started to use her connection to help other leaders rebuild their confidence. Another leader was able to recognize the point at which his energy threatened to dissipate, and instead learnt to re-anchor himself in his strong beliefs about himself and the work he had set out to do. He was also able to build on that deep self-awareness to help articulate the vision he had for his role, and through his heightened emotional presence engage his colleagues in a shared sense of the bigger contribution he wanted to make. In his words: 'I now realize that I need to bring and show more of myself at work. Otherwise I will not be able to connect with others.'

The act of recognizing when and how we can become trapped in debilitating patterns – endless loops of unproductive energy – and lose our sense of purpose and our unique value is a core capability of a touchpoint leader. As with many leaders, these patterns can be accompanied by an overwhelming sense of overload, a loss of energy, and doubt about personal direction and purpose. This in turn can lead to exhaustion, with its inevitable impact on the rest of the leader's life. It brings us to an interesting consideration of personal energy and power, and the need for each leader to fully develop and embody the personal values and meaning that govern the way in which he or she makes sense in the business. In this way resilience becomes re-formed as confidence in one's purpose and the capacity to use it as a set of guiding principles that serve as the leader's moral compass. This is a new form of resilience, one built on self-awareness and self-belief, constantly shaped by the context of belonging to a much bigger 'system' and connecting effectively with that system through multiple touchpoints.

Trust is critical in these cases – as is the willingness to be vulnerable and remain open to the learning that emerges – as we shall see in the next section. As an individual leader commits to the very personal journey of inquiring into his or her purpose and values the challenges and expectations of the business do not stand still. In some cases this has meant compromise – and in others has highlighted that an individual simply is not ready to take the risk. We have seen leaders unable to trust either the system or the people within it; this level of distrust feeding their isolation – in some ways protecting them from derailing but at the same time limiting their ability to be fully present as a leader. In these cases we work with their ability to develop a quality of attention that will feed their insights into the touchpoint: to pause, to notice and reflect, and then choose to make decisions to act. We refer to this approach as 'attentional',[4] encouraging our clients to work with data as it emerges, giving it a quality of attention that is very different from the very purposeful framing that often characterizes their work.

We therefore invite leaders to consider reviewing the contract they have with themselves, the contract to which they will hold themselves to account just as they hold themselves collectively to account as organizational leaders. And so we would encourage you to ask:

- How do I find a path through all the complexity and the pressures of my role, and still maintain an identity that has meaning for me?

- How can I be sure that I'm creating some real value for me, you and others?

- How honest am I being with myself and through the role I play?

- How can I work with the contradictions that might challenge my connections?

- How can I hold myself to account according to who I am... now?

CASE STUDY

John successfully worked with all of these questions and as a consequence took a huge step to rebalance his life. He was a very senior and well-respected executive, close to his CEO and playing an influential role in leading the business. He was very self-aware in many ways, and had begun to focus on a gap and tension in his life. All the connecting points (touchpoints) in his life appeared to be presenting a source of tension, which could have been a source for creativity for him but instead the size of the difference was so great that it was beginning to drain his energy. His hugely intentional drive was no longer working for him and he felt he needed to step out of his current situation before he could begin to address the tensions that were causing him to feel so torn apart. He also told parallel stories of personal health, wellbeing and fitness and knew that his life as it was could not be sustainable.

He displayed enormous courage and emotional honesty when he finally said: this is no longer working for me. And as he stepped out of a highly valued role he was determined to avoid the outstretched arms of the head-hunters who believed that his ongoing connection with them would be critical to his professional survival. He needed to step out of the role he felt he had become, describing it as if it might be a suit of armour. He was stepping into a restorative space – swapping a sense of sacrifice, being depleted, obeying the 'musts' and 'shoulds' of life to take time to explore what was really important to him – and the relationships he either selected or de-selected would be formative in that process.

We met him again about nine months after he took the decision to step out. His energy was fully restored, he was fit and healthy and exploring multiple new strands that were both intellectually and personally stimulating.

We recognize that business demands strong leadership, and in many cases that has been interpreted into a particular form of 'heroic' leadership. We are proposing that it is time to renegotiate the meaning of strength in this context. Rather than businesses needing 'heroic' leaders we believe that many people are now seeking leadership that is defined by its openness, someone they can connect with – and someone who knows how to nurture the energy that has the potential to galvanize businesses and communities to take collective and connected action.

Leadership is certainly about taking decisions that have consequence and leaders need to be prepared to stand and be counted, especially when it goes wrong – often living with consequences that have impact far beyond the economy of the individual business. We operate in a joined up global world where social and environmental impact is inextricably linked to economic behaviour. Generally leaders make decisions on imperfect information – working with what they know now and limited by learnt patterns of sense-making. Not all of these are either effective or useful. So how do we help develop the judgement, confidence and accountability that are so critical and which will help shape the touchpoint? And how do we ensure that those decisions are based on sound human values that have emerged from deep personal awareness of the individual leader? One leader, Peter, showed a determined courage to do just this.

CASE STUDY

Peter displayed an enormous sense of loyalty to his team leaders, founded on his own deep values of care and respect. He also operated within an organizational system that encouraged people to take risks – the only caveat being that if they failed at the task they demonstrate to others what they had learnt. He had reached a point in his career where he needed to decide whether he wanted to aim for a broader leadership role in the same business or look for a new opportunity outside the organization. A new global leader had recently taken over the business, making it a critical time to establish effective connections between the US-centric leadership and the regional leaders, and Peter recognized that he had an opportunity to proactively present himself as a candidate for the role – if indeed he decided to go for it.

At the same time there was a weakness in his local leadership team. One of his direct reports, Len, was struggling with a set of personal challenges but was fiercely loyal to both Peter and the business and had a long-established track record that had been somewhat blemished in the last few years. Karen was holding a critical role at the customer interface but was struggling to deliver. She was clearly in the wrong role but not yet ready to admit it to herself.

Peter had some big decisions to make – for himself, for these two direct reports and for the wider business. He needed to find the connective dialogue that would enable them all to feel affirmed and at the same time liberate them to move on. As he appeared to prevaricate there was huge risk to Peter – his strong values of caring and loyalty bringing him into tension with his US bosses just at a time when promotion was critical for him. He stood his ground. We worked with him to support Len and Karen in exploring what needed to happen for them – and they each in turn secured roles that played to their strengths. The confidence Peter communicated from taking this stance stood him in good stead and he is now the successful MD of the European business. When we spoke to him recently he was very clear on the value of his preserving his position, recognizing that the nature of his difference based on his own fundamental principles had enabled him to project a confidence and resilience that is now helping shape the touchpoint with his new boss.

In this story Peter gives us a clear example of how leadership can emerge at the touchpoint, grounded in a deep appreciation of both personal and collective values and held firmly to account by the principles that define it. We can draw three questions from the work:

1 What if all new leaders emerging across the organization were able to connect with their deeply held values in this way?

2 What insights might they bring to strategy development, and how might these 'new' voices express their understanding of the past and articulate their aspirations for the future?

3 And what if they were able to connect with and through their difference, avoiding any distortion of the difference in an attempt to integrate or smooth over?

Personal growth through interaction at the touchpoint

Learning with and through others

As we experience challenge and difference in our relationships we have huge possibilities of connection – and disconnection – and can clearly choose how we respond. Margaret Wheatley[5] talks about it as a chance to rediscover what it means to be human, to practise good human behaviours in connective dialogue. We describe it as a way in which the touchpoint can become catalytic, each new experience an opportunity to extend both the individual and collective capacity for knowing and helping extend each of the identities that have helped co-create it.

To make this happen leaders need to be reflective practitioners,[6] curious and able to hold a dynamic and dialogic space that allows them to learn and grow through connection with and through others. As their knowing shifts they need the courage to step back and tap into the power of their own narrative, telling and retelling their stories to fully realize the shift in their knowing. Not knowing is ok and useful, as is the capacity to explore both with intent and with attention – the first a very purposeful inquiry while the second is very much about noticing where the energy beckons. The reflective leader will oscillate between the two, noticing and appreciating the counterpoint and at the same time being able to generate trust – in themselves, in others and across the organization. In this way the touchpoint becomes a rich learning space, a way of keeping us at our learning edge.

These are some of the questions we would encourage you to ask yourself:

- How can I learn from my interaction with you... in ways that are reciprocal and generative?
- Which relationships have been most catalytic in my development?
- What might I as an individual learn about my effectiveness in relationship with others on behalf of the business?
- If I were to have access to one more relationship to help me deal with a current and significant challenge, what would that give me?

We encourage leaders to be curious about their potential to grow at every point of connection, and work with them to develop a constant awareness of the impact they have on others – and the impact others have on them. As we focus on working with these relational connections for the benefit of the business we also remind leaders that their understanding of everything in the past can also change, often so that they can no longer see the idea in the old way.

This means that leaders accept that they are constantly growing their wholeness through learning, that their identity is wider than one piece of knowledge – and that they accept the constant challenges to their knowing. For those leaders who have built their positions and reputations on being expert it can feel as if their whole sense of identity is being de-constructed, a theme we return to in Chapter 4. We encourage them to explore the developmental stages defined by Torbert and Rooke[7] where we can see a well-researched pattern of development that gives a frame to this need to let go of certainty. Torbert and Rooke map out seven action logics that help define a leader's dominant way of thinking, each one aligned to an increasing capacity to achieve corporate and individual performance. It's in the late stage action logics that we see the emergence of the effective transformational leader, defined by a capacity to exercise the power of mutual inquiry, vigilance and vulnerability for both the short and long term. Joiner and Josephs offer a similar development framework in their 2007 work on leadership agility.[8]

Stephen illustrates how these kinds of shifts in personal awareness can lead to much broader attentional shifts, and in his case irrevocably changed the way in which he connected with his colleagues. When we first met him his lack of 'other' awareness had been blocking his appointment to the executive team. During our work together he moved from holding a position of 'sole operator', for which he was highly valued and extremely successful, to become an executive with a much broader relational presence.

CASE STUDY

When we first met him Stephen was aiming for a position on the newly-formed executive team. He headed up a significant functional area of the business, and had acquired a reputation for keen negotiation. He was described as determined, single-focused and functionally expert by the CEO. These behaviours and characteristics were clearly valued and well-rewarded, but to achieve the coveted promotion he would need to develop a capacity for relationship-building, shared outcomes and connected working across functions. This represented a significant shift for him, challenging the very strengths he had developed while operating as a 'sole trader' and causing him to question what 'connected' might look and feel like for him.

It was difficult at first to fully appreciate the disconnected experiences his colleagues reported but we also recognized that there was something we weren't quite catching. We began to record the assumptions and beliefs that Stephen appeared to be holding, with the intention of helping him recognize where recurrent patterns might be impacting the quality of his connections with colleagues. As he continued to talk this framework of beliefs began to take on a very tangible presence, almost becoming an expression of the individual Stephen held himself to be.

Based on our understanding of Bill Torbert's work it seemed critical that Stephen develop an awareness of these deep-set beliefs. He had come into the development programme with a clear purpose, and with clear feedback from his peers, team and CEO that he needed to do something differently if he was to achieve his goal. We were unsure at this stage whether he had considered deep issues such as his identity, nor had we discussed yet the ways in which he might wish to develop as a leader. As with other clients working with similar questions we decided to use Marilee Goldberg's notions of 'Judger self' and 'Learner self'[9] to help him work it through. In *The Art of the Question* (1998, pp 147–8) Goldberg gives this description:

> The Judger Self orients itself to the world according to the belief that an individual should be able to achieve his version of what is right, good, correct, and acceptable in any particular arena of life, and at all times... the Judger Self places itself in a position of constantly seeking to confirm that it is right about its judgments. Any doubt about these standards or opinions might be experienced as dangerous by threatening to undermine or challenge the entire cognitive system upon which they are based.... The Learner Self is secure and fully self-accepting. Since it need not focus internally to find out if it's OK, it can afford to direct its attention externally to learn, connect, produce and create. The Learner Self recognizes that it makes choices constantly and this gives it a great deal of personal power. In taking responsibility for itself and its choices, the Learner Self garners the strength and possibilities that only this mindset can extend. It responds, rather than merely reacts, to whatever life throws its way.

Intuiting that Goldberg's concept might provide a useful framework for Stephen we shared it with him at the next meeting, along with a copy of the list of apparent beliefs and assumptions we'd made during the first session. Stephen appeared stunned as he acknowledged them as his. He read through the list and reflected for a very long time, before acknowledging that he was making sense of the world primarily from the perspective of a 'Judger self'.

One by one he described the choices he had made in his life, and was continuing to make. He began to add to the list of unhelpful beliefs he had accumulated over a lifetime, posing himself questions as he did so. As he structured his own inquiry we listened, noticing how the pace had slowed, appreciating his emotional courage and honesty and sharing some of the humour he was beginning to express. We sensed he was already beginning to free himself from a habitual and restrictive way of being and had started to explore the new choices open to him.

We worked together on this agenda for nearly a year. Whenever he became stuck he learnt to ask what his 'Learner self' might advise him to do. The only intervention was the questions. A couple of months before the end of the programme Stephen was successfully appointed to the position on the executive board. Just nine months later he was nominated as the CEO's future successor, and now has the next phase of his development plan to work on.

In this example we can track the specific and catalytic questions that helped shape the nature of the touchpoint that this leader was able to generate. These are the questions we refer to as generative, each formed from a quality of attention that enables us to intuitively frame a question that causes the client to shift his or her perspective. In Stephen's case we drew attention to the sense-making frame – or the lens through which he viewed the world – that was impacting his ability to connect.

Stephen learnt to observe himself in action,[10] noticing those moments when he was about to define his interactions with colleagues through a frame of 'I win, you lose' or in some cases a highly critical lens of judgement against his own criteria. His colleagues experienced the change, reporting through a 360-degree review that they found Stephen much warmer and more open to dialogue. By enabling his 'Learner self' Stephen was able to express his own capacity for 'not knowing', demonstrating a degree of humility that enabled him to ask for help.

Valuing the insights of vulnerability

Trust and respect are implicit in our relationships, helping create a connective space in which we can each be fully and emotionally present. And it takes courage, on all our parts, to avoid the temptation to smooth over and hasten to a premature resolution of the tension and discomfort that both threatens and defines the touchpoint.

Many leaders at first challenge us when we suggest that they should admit their vulnerability – to themselves as much as to others – and yet we know it's critical in developing the capacity to remain at their learning edge. This is the point at which they 'unknow' – and need to remain open to new and unanticipated possibilities. They can achieve it alone, through disciplined practices of reflection, self-inquiry and analysis, but we have found through our work that the greatest opportunity to tap into 'new' is as it emerges, live between people, at the touchpoint – at the point at which we interact and remain open to what might flow from the connection. To ensure this happens we have to be sure that the relationship is safe and that we can tolerate the risk. The risk of not-knowing and being drawn into premature certainty, the risk of caring for the homogeneity of the group and letting go of the challenge that would reinforce its difference and maximize the opportunity to learn, are both very real. Being different takes time and it takes courage to resist being driven to smooth over and establish certainty.

CASE STUDY

James had been working in the organization for just over three years, initially brought in to help integrate the work of the various leadership teams post-merger and more recently to support engagement with the new business vision. He was in charge of the overall programme plan, working alongside Anne who was in charge of the launch plan.

Anne had her own views on how they should proceed and expected to work with her own process and choices. The CEO knew exactly how he wanted things to work and depended on James to ensure it happened that way. The more the CEO insisted that things should be done his way, the more Anne took an entrenched position. Frustrated by his inability to influence her he asked James to take over the launch plan.

The tension between these three threatened to derail the launch of the programme but they seemed unable to correct their course. The CEO expected his direction to be followed, Anne expected to have the freedom to apply the insights from her own experience, and James wanted to do the job he perceived he'd been brought in to do. There was very little connection between them, they knew very little about each other, and certainly hadn't taken the time to share their perspectives or motivations for the task in hand. It was James's intolerance for the level of friction being generated that finally cut through the tension and caused them to reassess their potential to work together.

He and Anne had been in a particularly frustrating meeting, where neither was prepared to cede ground. They had maintained their politeness for over two hours. James described what happened next as the most shocking but valuable experience of his professional life. He simply let go of everything that he had been trying to control – and in that moment not only allowed his frustration to have free rein but more importantly allowed himself to become vulnerable. And that was the point at which they connected. Anne experienced his passion for the work for the first time and was able to loosen her hold on what needed to be done. By liberating his own pent-up emotion James understood that it was Anne's passion for the business that was driving her certainty and began to explore what he could learn from it. They both acknowledged their vulnerability and for the first time learnt to affirm each other's difference.

We recognize that the dominant paradigm indicates that we should not show vulnerability as leaders because it could be seen to be a sign of weakness. One leader we worked with frequently told his team that the opposite is true – that it is a sign of strength to say 'I don't know' or to ask for help. It is this willingness to show that we are not all-knowing and all-powerful that is so necessary for both un-learning and learning. In our work we put the attention on vulnerability as a capacity for learning.

However, we often see tough behaviour used as a mask for vulnerability. We have worked with a number of leaders who bring to their relationships a fear of being exposed as inadequate or inferior. Such leaders might see relationships as being about winning or losing, in which they project win-lose motives onto those with whom they interact. Some find it difficult to fully trust others because of a fear that they will be let down or defeated. Such deep-seated patterns can manifest themselves as aggressive or directive behaviour to others, and are often accompanied by an avoidance of conversations that might properly face up to and explore challenging or conflicting positions. In these situations we find that standing back from this pattern of behaviour, connecting with the emotions underpinning it and understanding its unintended consequences can help leaders start to explore the choices available to them if they move away from this win-lose mindset.

Once leaders can work with their vulnerability they can co-create the exploratory space that helps connect people, helps make the touchpoint its most creative by understanding what it takes to co-create a dialogic space, and posing their questions from their difference in such a way that it is generative. We tested the proposition with a client based in the Middle East, curious to hear the challenges he might identify from a very different context:

When you overlay global with cultural then the quality of relationships certainly becomes significant. And of course that spark point of contact can be negative as well as positive... Our world is very task-focused. The starting-point is anchored in lots of testosterone: we know how to do it, and then we run up against market differences, etc. The motto is 'get the job done' – and so we find a few people of the type who can deliver.

What's significant here is the emphasis on 'knowing how to do it'. Expertise and resolution are key – and we would not challenge that as an essential way to get business done. However, it does raise some specific questions around being expert at the same time as 'not knowing'. So how do we reconcile these apparently intractable differences?

CASE STUDY

We observed this tension played out in a significant global company when a new CEO was appointed. His predecessor had established his reputation on being at the centre of all decision making, his authority firmly rooted in his capacity to dig deep into the business and provide challenge where he observed uncertainty. Although clearly effective when measured solely on historical business results, this style of leadership had over time impacted the ability of his executive team to take their own positions at the helm of the business, and their capacity to take the lead had been severely depleted. Performance had begun to slip and this regime of leadership was unable to deliver the level of transformation that the company needed now. The new CEO demonstrated a very different style and that in itself presented a challenge. He was highly participative, reflective and asked questions of the executives to help catalyse their ownership of the necessary decisions. He both wanted and needed them to take the lead, to drive the business with purpose and energy, but they were temporarily unable to step up to what was being asked of them, and in turn criticized the CEO for being indecisive.

Through pausing and seeing the reflexive pattern that he had adopted they were able to see that, as resourceful and highly able leaders, they now had far more choices available to them as they responded to the new manager – not just win versus lose. They started to explore other more creative ways of developing a constructive relationship with him, drawing on a new, more grounded sense of themselves.

Being comfortable with not knowing

Pace and risk constantly appear as counter-arguments to this connective form of leadership, and in turn could threaten an emerging capacity for creativity and innovation. We hear so much about the need to accelerate – in how we make decisions, in how we plan, in how we deliver – so that pace is very often a subject of debate. We believe that this need for pace is both a reaction to not knowing, and an assumption that the next action might bring the answer if we can just be quick enough. We often see a nervousness based on the belief that if leaders don't act fast enough they might risk giving the impression that they're uncertain. We've seen this across clients in several sectors and have remarked on the number of leaders who do not see challenge as an exchange of learning. Instead they see it as an opportunity to prove that they are right.

Some leaders have suggested that this form of leadership is most open to challenge when crisis hits. They suggest that when you need to work at break-neck speed to sort things out you can't have a caucus – people in the organization crave leadership at that time, and that leadership is expected to be strong and decisive. But it's dangerous to focus everything on the leader, because he or she can fail. We can all identify prominent leaders who have been absolutely not right on occasions – but thankfully most of them have been prepared to permit challenge and have changed their minds. But it's the way in which the challenge is received that is critical. In one client's words:

> If a leader transmits that he or she cannot be challenged then it is likely
> that the executives and leaders around them will turn off those parts
> of their brains. The touchpoint is switched off. They no longer come up
> with ideas – just as the crisis needs them. People give up because they
> won't take the knock-back.

Interestingly, in this client's example the CEO was given the feedback and was shocked to realize that this was in fact the consequence of something he was doing or how he was being.

We also know of CEOs who won't make challenge easy and explain their approach as coming from a hard school that says we must jump through endless hoops of fire. We see this very clearly in Chapter 4 when we explore some of the work we have done with professional partnership firms – their high need to be expert a serious challenge to their ability to engage dialogically with their clients. But is this really the most effective way to nurture the creative tension in the organization? If you yourself send out these messages, are you sure you're fully developing the collective talent for growth and innovation? Do you know how it feels to be at that touchpoint? And are you prepared to accept that there might be a need to be a little more honest about your own vulnerability, and to find an effective way of expressing it? Can you say as a leader that you don't have the answers?

It's certainly challenging to create a space in which you can be present as a strong participative leader who likes to be part of the fray. It's not an easy balance – to invite challenge and be open to new possibilities while holding the expectation that you need to know. It's also difficult to express a view in this context without it being heard as a definite position and to invite others to question and debate.

So, do you need to give explicit permission? One of our clients found that she had to do this – and avoided facilitating her own away-days so that she could reinforce her intention of playing a co-creating role. But it wasn't easy to convince some of her team and she struggled to get them to fully participate. We also know that even while a leader may intend to be more collaborative he or she may have to work hard to shift the habitual leadership patterns that have served him or her well as a more directive leader. It requires constant self-reflection, feedback and practice to change these patterns, especially where the prevailing culture places emphasis on exerting tight control to deliver tangible results.

The art comes from within the leader, born out of a deep insight into how your own sense-making works and having the capacity to pay attention to the dialogue as it happens. And dialogue itself is an art,[11] demanding that we listen cleanly and without applying judgement, that we fully respect the frame of the other and that we respond in a way that is co-constructive and helps generate new knowing. These qualities are highlighted in the next section as we explore the qualities of exchange and reciprocity at the touchpoint, and are evidenced further in Chapter 5 as we share stories of clients who begin to form the qualities of connective learning at the touchpoint as a critical behaviour of collaborative leadership.

Developing a relational perspective

Engaging through dialogue

In the first part of this chapter we expanded on our basic premise that the art of Touchpoint Leadership starts with our own self-awareness and our awareness of others. It is this capacity to bring our 'true' and constantly developing selves into the human network of relationships that enables each of us to realize our difference in effective and positive ways. In this part of the chapter we look at the capacity of the leader to release energy and power through his or her interaction with others, drawing differences together in a form of dialogue that both respects each leader's autonomous identity and recognizes that interdependence can only be achieved if we are able to engage from that autonomous position in a way that is connective and co-creative.

In my PhD work[11] I explored the connective power of dialogue as a form of creative exchange that could enable personal and collective transformation. I developed seven principles as the defining qualities of this kind of dialogue, which I later developed further in an article published in the January 2011 edition of the *Educational Journal of Living Theories*.[12] We have grouped them together here as:

- Valuing and encouraging questions that open up new possibilities and allow unanticipated insights to emerge.

- Facilitating a deep reflective space for individuals and teams to step back and consider simple but profound questions of what matters and has meaning for them.

- Suspending judgement even when hearing contradictions to our deeply held values, vision and purpose.

- Being prepared to let go of habitual ways of thinking and allowing the dialogue to help co-create new frames and meaning to flow.

The principles are based on the work of Isaacs,[13] Bohm[14] and Marshall[15] and help define a way of working with individuals and groups who are seeking to find ways of connecting and working positively with their diverse perspectives and contributions. Based on this earlier work we've further developed our insights into the qualities of exchange and energy that are generated at the touchpoint, noticing when the connection is so generative that it catalyses energy to flow – and at other times is almost toxic. Understanding these differences is critical in enabling the touchpoint to become a living source of energy.

In an article in *Harvard Business Review*, Groysberg and Slind[16] point to the need for leaders to move away from directive and top-down leadership models to one where they relate to their people in conversation, deploying intimacy and interactivity to engage people in active dialogue. These authors, like us, believe that mental and emotional proximity – the ability to see the many people in the organization as real people rather than an anonymous mass – is more important than physical proximity.

The following story illustrates what can happen when a group of individuals fail to engage in this way, and instead fall into unhelpful habits of needing to know rather than exploring through dialogue. What should have been a rich and creative exchange, working with the multiple touchpoints in the room, became trapped in a question/answer frame.

CASE STUDY

A few years ago a member of one of the major business schools invited us to take part in a module he was running as part of the MBA programme. It was a two-day module on consultancy, with participants drawn from across a very broad spectrum of businesses. He asked us to join the group as both practising consultants and as senior industry representatives. We had met previously on an experimental workshop exploring the potential of dialogue as a learning process.

He was keen to open up the dialogic possibilities of the group and set up a 'fishbowl' approach, with five chairs placed inside the main circle of chairs and representatives of five break-out groups seated in each of the chairs. A sixth chair was then placed inside the circle and left empty and inviting for anyone who wished to join the discussion. The rest of the participants, including ourselves, sat in a larger circle of chairs that surrounded the inner circle.

As we listened we were struck by two things – the 'telling' propensity of the group and the lack of inquisitiveness. We were fascinated by some of the standpoints some of them were taking, particularly their apparent condemnation of 'polite conversation' within organizations. One of us joined the group and immediately sensed a feeling of anticipation as they appeared to wait for her to speak. She opened with a question, intending it to be catalytic. Someone replied. She asked another one. Someone else replied. It was as if they assumed they should find the 'right' answer to the question. The energy level of the group began to drop, and there appeared to be some anger and frustration. People left the group and others joined. She sensed the change, stepped out of the group and re-joined the outer circle.

The facilitator called a halt to the exercise and after a short break we reconvened to discuss what had happened in the session. There were comments about the impact of one of us joining the group, of the way in which the group had turned to make her the focal point. But more significantly there were comments about the impact of her questions. They had all felt uncomfortable and one likened the experience to being interviewed. We asked them to reflect on what had happened for them to respond in that way but they were not prepared to explore the possibility that they had in fact played a role at the point of connection.

Later, two of the clients approached us and thanked us for our input. They were particularly keen to pursue notions of politeness and respect in their organizations and felt we had demonstrated behaviour that personified their beliefs. They had also appreciated our intention to help catalyse the group's capacity for inquiry through our carefully formed questions but also recognized that something had blocked it. Another, a young man already working as a consultant for one of the major professional services firms, summed it up very clearly. He warned us that such 'soft' behaviour did not go hand in hand with 'making big bucks', and that it was essential for consultants to always have the answers.

This last comment proved to have an increasing significance for us when we later worked with a series of professional services firms, providing support as they made every effort to change the underlying assumption that the consultant must be expert. We share some of these examples in Chapter 4.

In an article written in the *Financial Times* (24 August 2010) entitled: 'Kindness can be the hardest word of all', Tom Peters put forward this proposition:

> *If people and relationships are the* sine qua non *of enterprise success, and I flatly assert that they are, then decency, thoughtfulness and the likes of attentive listening should know no peers in the management*

canon. I will stake my professional reputation on it: 'soft' is indeed 'hard', and Kindness = Repeat business = Profit.

His notion of 'attentive listening' has particular resonance when we reflect on this example of a group of emerging leaders and consultants who, in the main, had not yet reached the point of development at which they would begin to value the qualities of connection that would sustain the business models on which they depended. Many of the participants will now hold senior positions, possibly even in the same organizations. Although it is not possible to re-assemble the group and explore how experience has potentially altered the quality of their dialogue, we can ask this question more broadly: what if, by developing our individual capacity for dialogue and inquiry, we were able to catalyse a level of exchange with others that could propel our collective progress and growth in connected and joined up ways?

When we tested this with a group of clients one offered this response:

I don't think anyone would disagree with the premise. I'm sure many CEOs and senior leaders would say they're trying to do that all the time. Many case studies of businesses might say that the strengths of relationships and working at the senior level have really power-housed the business. I don't doubt that at all. But if a business finds itself with lots of short-term problems it will need lots of strength and self-confidence to stick to that. It's so tempting to step into 'tell and do' mode.

The response is a timely reminder that context can be hugely influential on the touchpoint, and it is all too easy to find reasons why we might act autonomously. The test is this: are we making a positive impact on the outcomes of the business?

The catalytic value of exchange

By engaging with these dialogic qualities at the touchpoint, and understanding how individuals can help generate this catalytic consciousness,[17] leaders have the capacity to both liberate and engage the energy in the system – helping build the channels for its flow and letting go of anything that might otherwise block it in the complex mix of personal behaviour or beliefs. More important, they can help build a connective strength that will underpin their organizational resilience and provide the foundations for generating long-term value by focusing very firmly on their capacity to co-create at the touchpoint. And that co-creation depends on sustaining the qualities of exchange and reciprocity, pushing aside the transactional nature that is characteristic of so many relationships and instead becoming the point at which full leadership is realized – the dialogic qualities of listening, trusting, suspending judgement and letting go[18] critical to its impact.

One business developed this capacity as a key differentiator. The business is built on the capacity to deliver global engineering projects, pulling together teams from across geographies and from across skill sets. It identified the need to facilitate frequent cross-pollination and placed champions at the interfaces, individuals who are selected to be 'floating touchpoints'. One manager worked in India for a month and spent time explaining, working alongside and training the local teams. He found the dynamics fascinating – observing different levels of professional competences as well as cultural differences.

He described these roles as 'flexible links' – people who are able to flex the differences. They hold the show together, hold the constructive tension and at the same time resolve the differences. They hold a position between opposing views, facilitating through the qualities of dialogue and so becoming the exchange points in the space between the two partnering groups. The individual positions don't totally change, especially in the short term, but the relational touchpoint does. He's also very clear in defining the behaviours and attitudes of the candidates for these roles:

We can't disseminate the consciousness for change to all – we need to find someone who can communicate it without being authoritarian... someone who can help them discover what it means to them... They have coaching skills, international experience, experience of living outside their own environment, possibly multilingual... people who are not too opinionated about social and moral values. They need to ask 'why' and 'what can I learn from it'. They need to be non-judgmental and recognize that both are equally right. They must recognize that morals are simply different and exist in different places. But, we can run

up against problems if they become too homogenous. They lose
that spark of constructive tension... and so a balance has to be struck.
I therefore see these flexible links as allowing the full force of the energy
exchange in effective ways.

We experienced something similar in co-writing this book and realized at a very early stage that we had to explore how we could
hold onto our own discovery space as well as explore each other's,
enabling our co-creation to happen in what we began to call our
'weaving space'. We understood it as first innovating singly, and then
collectively needing a dialogic space in which we could co-create
'new' insights that neither of us would have managed alone.

This also caused us to reflect on the similar tensions experienced
when working in and with global teams. It's important that leaders
and teams across the geographies can fully realize their difference,
and particularly where it is critical for success in the local market. At
the same time they're expected to contribute to the collective 'knowing' of the business, and in most cases that sits centrally as a core
capacity of the business. Just at the moment when the business makes
collective sense of its experiences it seems that there has to be a level
of trust and confidence that any one area of the business won't go off
at a completely different tangent – the qualities of the relationship
holding a space within which individual leaders can fully realize the
tension and spark of the touchpoint as a rich source of insight for
both local and global operations. And of course that 'knowing' will
continue to shift as various parts of the organization continue to integrate their 'expert' insights with their emerging dialogic insights – as
long as the quality of exchange is maintained. Without it the 'knowing' becomes fixed and sits on the corporate shelf as 'knowledge', a
snapshot in time.

We know that where leaders and leadership teams are able to liberate energy at the touchpoint they are able to make remarkable connections. In one company a senior leader described the connections
in the team as giving him the energy to keep going. He felt that they
cared for each other, and for themselves as a team. That mattered to
him. In his words: 'It builds some conscious, additional loyalties... It
was a team that cared – if you were unwell, looking stressed – it

would take you aside. There was still nervousness about displaying that upwards to the boss. But laterally it worked.'

We've also heard a similar assessment of the qualities of connection expressed by a newly appointed NED (non-executive director) of a major UK firm. He described the role of the NED as needing resilience, loyalty, empathy and deep listening and saw the need to balance connective relationships that held all that together in a self-respecting, mutual place where vulnerability enabled learning. Trust was fundamental to sustaining this quality of exchange – and his experience was built on integrity and an authentic embodiment of personal values. In both of these cases there was a deeply held trust that enabled the connections to happen.

CASE STUDY

Around the same time we worked with an individual leader who appeared to challenge the qualities of exchange implicit in this relational model of leadership, and essential if leaders are to fully realize the potential of the touchpoint. Matthew was a 'new' leader who appeared to hold a belief that the organization had a duty to offer him the increasingly broader roles that would give him the opportunity to grow. He had fully engaged with his own purpose but struggled to understand that the need was reciprocal – that the system also needed him to engage with the collective purpose and thereby play a much bigger role in its realization. Until he could hold the two in dialogue – a sense of his own purpose alongside the organization's purpose – he would continue to reflect a quality of disconnection that his colleagues found discouraging. He received the feedback as part of the debrief from an unsuccessful promotion panel.

Matthew was in the early stages of understanding the principles of exchange. He needed to trust, be confident in his ability to engage with mutual benefit, and to move from holding a belief that relationships were a political 'game' to one that would serve him much more robustly. He genuinely wanted the opportunity to co-create and learn, but for as long as he engaged in this transactional way he could not be fully present in ways that would generate reciprocal value and engender that quality of connection that his colleagues needed to feel.

We explored with him what it meant to have impact in a global firm, how he might grow his connectivity by actually letting go of some of his certainty and opening himself up to unlearning much of what he assumed about the 'rules of getting on'. He began to redefine his relationships as a dynamic source of value and energy – and at the end of our work together had shifted his governing belief from 'Well, if that's the game I'll jump through hoops... as long as they deal fairly with me' to a readiness to trust his colleagues sufficiently to begin to explore how they might generate value together.

In describing this quality of the touchpoint as one of 'exchange' we are therefore seeking to emphasize the way in which the touchpoint is realized as an ability to catalyse co-creation and mutual growth. This not only depends on the readiness to engage with dialogic intent – suspending judgement and premature closure by remaining curious and open to new insights that might emerge – but also on the ability to remain present with all the vulnerability of a learner and a prepared-ness to shift a sense of self in relation to the shifts in another.

Looking forward

In the next chapter we put much more focus on this relational aspect of our identity as leaders, and share insights from a number of pivotal relationships that have had a significant impact on both the individuals concerned and on the working groups in which they participated. As we move towards this focus on specific relationships we encourage you to reflect on your own, and to consider the following questions:

- To what extent are you prepared to be open to new ideas and influences?
- How vulnerable are you prepared to be?
- How far are you willing to give up some of your need for control to develop a stronger shared leadership with others in the business?
- Which connections have been most catalytic in your own development?
- Which connections are pivotal to your performance now?

Notes

1 Jack Whitehead developed this concept of 'living contradiction' as a way of helping frame the tensions researchers and educators were expressing as they articulated the principles of their professional practices within the constraints of the systems within which they lived and worked. It also provided a rich seem of energy and insight for his own PhD thesis, 'How do I improve my practice? Creating a discipline of education through educational inquiry' (PhD thesis 1999, University of Bath, **http://www.actionresearch.net/jack.shtml**).

2 Graham Lee (2003) *Leadership Coaching: From personal insights to organizational excellence* (London, CIPD).

3 Rosenwald and Ochberg pose this question: 'Can a person by telling her (sic) story rescue her understanding from both accidental and formal self-misunderstanding and inadvertent self-misrepresentation? Can life stories be opened up, as well as cramped, in the telling?' in their book *Storied Lives: The cultural politics of self-understanding* (London, Yale University Press, 1992).

4 The use of 'attentional' in this way was developed by Jacqui Scholes-Rhodes in her PhD thesis (2002) to differentiate between the purposeful qualities of those dialogues that are predicated on a predefined purpose and scope and those dialogues and inquiries that emerge due to a much deeper sense of their significance (**http://www.actionresearch.net/living/rhodes.shtml**).

5 Margaret J Wheatley (2002) *Turning to one Another: Simple conversations to restore hope to the future* (San Francisco, Berrett-Koehler).

6 Donald A Schon (1991) *The Reflective Practitioner* (Aldershot, Ashgate).

7 Bill Torbert and David Rooke (2005) Seven transformations of leadership, *Harvard Business Review*, April. The authors draw on 25 years' consulting experience and collaboration with psychologist Susanne Cook-Greuter to present a typology of leadership based on the way managers personally make sense of the world around them.

8 Joiner and Josephs respond to the global challenges of accelerating change and growing complexity and interdependence with a leadership development framework built on the qualities of leadership agility, described by them as representing the capacity 'to take wise and effective action amid complex, rapidly changing conditions... an intentional, proactive stance'. See *Leadership Agility: Five levels of mastery for anticipating and initiating change* (San Francisco, Jossey-Bass, 2007).

9 Marilee C Goldberg (1998) *The Art of the Question* (New York, Wiley & Sons).

10 Donald A Schon (1995) Knowing-in-action: The new scholarship requires a new epistemology, *Change*, 27–34, Nov–Dec.

11 In her PhD thesis 'From the inside out', Jacqui Scholes-Rhodes develops a combined practice of dialogue and inquiry and presents it as 'a creative art of inquiry' (PhD thesis 2002, University of Bath, **http://www.actionresearch.net/living/rhodes.shtml**).

12 *The Educational Journal of Living Theories* (EJOLTS) publishes the accounts of practitioner-researchers from a wide range of global, social, cultural and professional contexts that explain their educational influences in their own learning, in the learning of others and in the learning of social formations. The journal focuses on personal journeys and collaborative pathways that explain educational influences in learning in terms of values, skills and understandings that the researcher believes carries hope for the future. Jacqui Scholes-Rhodes's paper can be found at **http://ejolts.net/node/180**.

13 William Isaacs (1999) *Dialogue and the Art of Thinking Together* (New York, Currency Doubleday).

14 David Bohm (1996) *On Dialogue* (London, Routledge).

15 Judi Marshall, Self-reflective inquiry practices, in P Reason and H Bradbury (eds) *Handbook of Action Research; Participative inquiry and practice* (London, Sage).

16 Groysberg, B and Slind, M (2012) Leadership is a conversation, *Harvard Business Review*, June.

17 The expression 'catalytic consciousness' has been built from an understanding of David Bohm's, specifically *Unfolding Meaning, A weekend of dialogue with David Bohm* (1985) in which he puts forward the notion that dialogic connectivity may engender a quality of consciousness that itself will engender the formation of human relationships.

18 William Isaacs sets out these four as the defining qualities of dialogue (see note 13).

Pivotal relationships – creating value within the organization

03

Organizations behave like a body which has learnt how to repel a cold. They implant people at senior levels and then respond to them as if they were a form of virus – either a good virus that invades the body and generates mutation and makes it better, like a vaccination, or if it can't find a way of working or changing the body in a positive way then they're pretty good at spitting them right back out again, at speed. Underestimate that at your peril! **(EXTRACT FROM A CONVERSATION WITH A SENIOR EXECUTIVE)**

In this chapter we put the focus on the co-creation of value at the touchpoint itself, tracking relationships within the business that both generate and block the flow of energy at the point at which they connect. We explore critical touchpoints within the business, illustrating how they have the potential to provide energy, coherence and sustainable growth to the collaborative enterprise, while at the same time always carrying the possibility of disruption if the attention or intent is lost. We evidence how these touchpoints are pivotal to the success and growth of the business.

We also start to demonstrate how an integrated and systemic approach to building relationships, and more significantly the touchpoints that give those relationships connectivity and energy, can enhance an organization's capacity to grow and adapt in response to both current and emerging business issues. We illustrate how positive energy can be developed and sustained through the frictions that are generated by difference and evidence how the business can see difference as an opportunity for change and creativity rather than a block to innovation. We share examples of locked-in potential, exploring how leaders can act to liberate such trapped-in capacity by bringing attention to the individual, relational and systemic patterns involved and by addressing their own needs to deep-dive and invade the very space that has potential to generate touchpoint energy.

Starting with the assumption that organizations are constructed of layer upon layer of relationships we demonstrate how leaders and teams have developed collective and connected action at the touchpoint in three interrelated ways by:

1 Focusing on connecting difference in a way that also respects and reinforces their difference.

2 Igniting connective energy to open up the possibilities for collective action.

3 Bringing attention to the relational qualities of the space between people and groups.

We build on the concepts of exchange and dialogue introduced in Chapter 2 and demonstrate how 'new' leadership is generative, affirmative and liberating. In this way leaders are able to work with fluid forms of knowing and are open to the possibility of bringing energy and coherence to their businesses by engendering creativity at multiple points of connection. We focus on the space between people and groups, paying attention to the enablers of positive energy that help achieve collective and individual action and encouraging the development of a dialogic interface that can hold aspects of difference in a connective development pattern.

In all of the examples we share we are struck by the common issues faced by these leaders as they realized that to increase their impact and influence they must begin to let go of the controls and frameworks that had supported them up to this point in their careers. In Chapter 2 we referred to the action logics of Torbert and Rooke[1] as a means of identifying the developmental stage a leader might have reached, the criteria of the 'expert' leader giving way to the qualities of collaboration and relational value as a leader moves into the later development stages. Joiner and Josephs[2] offer a similar model through their work, responding to the global challenges of accelerating change, growing complexity and interdependence with a leadership development framework built on the qualities of leadership agility. When leaders reach the post-heroic stages of development in this framework they begin to grow their commitment to collaborative relationships and develop their capacity to transform conflict into mutually beneficial solutions.

Throughout the chapter we will share examples of how leaders have achieved similar changes in their own leadership work, and how Touchpoint Leadership expands on this capacity to enable the value of friction by developing a facility for mutual and dialogic engagement that brings respect and openness to the point of connection.

Connecting and reinforcing difference

Freeing the ability to act

When talking to a senior leader about the potential challenges that can arise when seeking to connect difference across business and organizations, she shared this perspective:

> It reminds me that some women love to be told how different they are to men – and I am convinced that this is missing the point. It creates greater disconnection by fostering prejudice and excuses... This is a potentially disabling way of holding our difference – and therefore missing the possibilities for creating new types of leadership in organizations through creating new types of touchpoint experiences.

It's a powerful comment that draws into relief not only the tension that can be generated at the point of connection between different people and groups, but also how easy it is to reject the very challenge that has been recognized as critical to the future success of the business. We have only to track the number of programmes that seek to address aspects of difference, such as ethnic or gender diversity, to see evidence that this is a widespread issue.

We see the accentuation of difference wherever we look in the businesses around us. We have often been asked to help where relationships within teams have broken down and where leaders no longer have the ability to see with objective eyes what has led to the fragmentation. In some instances a relationship tension sparked by a tussle between control and autonomy has led to a pattern of avoidance between two leaders that has rippled out into divisive competition between the teams that reported to them. What started with two people's inability to work with their different needs and perspectives in a connected way developed, through an unchallenged pattern of assumption, imagined bad intent and separation, into a major block to the productivity of a whole division or business.

Our world is incredibly rich in difference. In our view, globalization isn't about creating a homogeneous world but about developing the art of holding the difference in a dialogic and enriching way. Our purpose in developing touchpoint leaders therefore is not to encourage the smoothing over of difference but to hold the moment at which the friction and/or tension is ignited and in that space co-create newness by learning and connecting. It's in this dialogic space that we have the opportunity to enable the emergence of profound new thinking, to generate connections that catalyse energy and develop the capacity to co-create reciprocal value which is in turn sustained by the capacity to co-inquire and learn.

Without this awareness and intent we can inadvertently block the very dialogue and understanding necessary for change to happen. These blocks in turn can very quickly become the reality of an organization or community, phrased so familiarly as 'that's not how we do it around here' or 'that doesn't fit with our culture' and evident time and time again as we come across 'stuck' behaviours and thinking in our clients.

In the next section we look at how we have worked with such blocks that have developed between management levels, the second story illustrating how dialogue helped find a channel for connecting constructively across the divide that had developed.

The positive power of affirmative dialogues

CASE STUDY

Many years ago we were having dinner with a group of senior leaders in an international business. As the conversation developed we became acutely aware that there was a strong theme of blaming upwards. The leaders present were bitter at some of the changes that had occurred and had fallen into a pattern of holding the global leader accountable. We were suddenly struck by the absurdity of a team of very senior leaders complaining at their own powerlessness. We asked them, 'How do you think your teams would view the conversation you are having now?' A ripple of embarrassment went round the room.

Gradually, one of the group started to suggest the possibility that they could open up a conversation to explore their concerns directly with their international boss.

It is not unusual to find whole teams and layers of management encouraging their own disempowerment in the way described here, by failing to consider the pressures of their own leadership and attributing bad intent to their actions (we come back to this in Chapter 5). The result can be a passivity that prevents the kind of dialogue that would enable creative resolution of the issues they face. The following story illustrates how we can free up this kind of 'stuckness' by paying attention to the nature of the question we ask, engaging in a dialogic process that helps move the reality to one that is both powerful and resourceful and puts the focus firmly on being affirmative.

CASE STUDY

The executive and his team were using a series of workshops to support their interventions as they took on leadership of the cross-company transformation. In the first workshop they had made some very powerful connections through sharing their personal stories, and had co-generated a quality of energy that had helped them become a cohesive and coherent team. During this second workshop, when they were keen to move on to action, something significant arose for them in the form of the questions they were asking and which were clearly keeping them disconnected from the global leader's intent.

We began the second day by establishing just what it was that needed their attention. The team's relationship with the global leader was top of their list. In the previous meeting they had experienced and articulated their collective power while taking a stance against his direction – and although helpful in the microcosm of the team's dynamics it was clearly unhelpful in the systemic space where they needed to have impact and influence. The tension they were holding was potentially creating a disconnection at the very point at which they needed to generate positive and focused energy.

We started with a blank flipchart and invited each of them to form the question that would catalyse their action planning and move them on. We recorded each of the questions as they were articulated, each a slight variation of the previous one but still clearly expressed from a similar perspective and position. This team was expressing its solidarity through its ongoing disconnection with their leader who clearly held a very different perspective from their own. The questions were about compromise, about colluding in something that didn't feel right to them, about remaining in opposition – and continued to build on their original assumption that their global leader's direction was wrong.

After about 20 minutes or so we paused, and asked the team to reflect on the pattern of their questioning. It was clearly uncomfortable for them to move at this slowing pace but it seemed a very rich source of understanding for them. They began to comment on a sense of conflict reinforced by their questions. They noticed the tension they were holding as they took a position of opposition. There were more pauses. We wondered whether they were stuck and respected their silence. One member of the team, a young woman, hadn't spoken up to this point. She suddenly spoke with enormous confidence: 'You know, we *can* be in control; we can *lead* this.'

There was even more silence in the room. The next question the team formed reverberated with her energy: 'So, how can we *support* the global leader to achieve success for the organization and *still* hold our different and challenging position?'

Their sense of liberation was expressed in this one question. Her intervention had powerfully shifted their perspective; they were no longer in opposition, disempowered by feelings of frustration and weary with the constant pushing back. They had moved alongside the global perspective, co-created a space of connection and alignment – the qualities of the touchpoint transformed in their reframing of the relationship. They added in more colour on the flipchart: 'by being in control of the agenda, by having shared clarity, by being aligned behind a common intent'.

There was no hint of compromise or smoothing over their difference – instead they had identified a dialogic way in which they could hold both positions and realize the creativity of the energy catalysed at the touchpoint.

This team were prepared to learn and to create a connective focus by engaging with the very difference that had previously threatened to weaken them and at worst derail them. In Chapter 5 we return to a story in which senior leaders intentionally shifted the conversation with their high-potential leaders as a way of enhancing their ability to succeed them in the business. But there are also examples of leadership teams who have not been able to achieve this dialogic engagement with a resulting negative impact on the business. In one case a CEO deliberately surrounded himself with a sub-set of leaders he regarded as being in his own mould in an attempt to bridge the gap he perceived between himself and the dominant talent base in the company. This homogeneous group were unable to generate the necessary touchpoint in the business and even though it was clear that a major project was not going to schedule there was no dialogic place in which to explore it and learn and adjust.

Figure 3.1 on page 92 illustrates the pattern that can emerge when this connective space is missing.

Risks inherent in developing a 'buffer' role

One client, a global leader in a project-based business, suggested that there might be cases where we need to create a third-party role to nurture the touchpoint. However, he had also seen first-hand the risks inherent in such a strategy and shared his own story with us. In leading a business that needed to find effective ways of connecting the activities of a project design team based in the UK with an implementation team based in India, he had explored the potential benefit of creating 'flexible touchpoint' roles between the two operations. These roles were filled by individuals who displayed high levels of adaptability and a strong tolerance for ambiguity. Although some had flourished in the roles, others had failed. Those who failed had demonstrated the same deep insights as their successful counterparts,

FIGURE 3.1   Creating connections – bottom-up and top-down

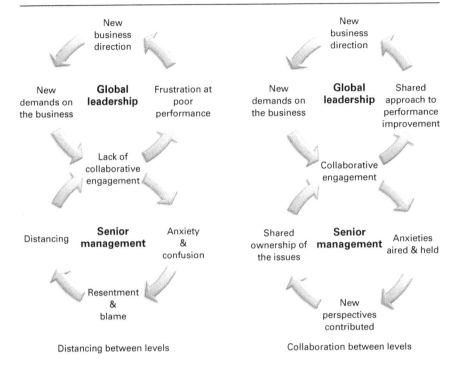

but instead of drawing on them to facilitate the connection, they had absorbed the difference and failed to help create a new, dialogic space that would have engendered creativity and insight and realize the very differences they were meant to affirm.

The ability to respect and hold difference, rather than absorb it, is a particular challenge for leaders during times of major organizational change. A leader needs to remain connected to his or her team members in a way that will sustain optimum performance. He needs to determine how much information and guidance to pass on to his team to ensure their active engagement, while at the same time trying to manage the impact of the stress that could be caused by constant changes. These changes can be destabilizing and the team may have little influence over them. How the leader acts in such situations can determine the nature of the connection that is created between the top of the business and those levels lower down.

The way in which leaders manage and communicate information is a defining aspect of leadership within any business, and varies widely in different organizational cultures. These differences are made obvious in a merger or acquisition where the norms of the legacy companies may have encouraged different approaches to the leader role. We have noted such a contrast where professional services organizations, based on a partnership governance structure in which strategic issues are shared relatively openly with professional staff, have merged with stock exchange listed companies, where the power structure is more hierarchical and communication influenced by concerns about investor perceptions on the share price. Each legacy organization views the other's approach as inappropriate – one as too free with information, lacking in managerial authority and accountability and spreading unnecessary anxiety; the other as over-hierarchical and controlled and breeding mistrust through secretiveness.

As the pressures on the business become more severe, leaders need the interpersonal insight to stand back from the changing dynamics that 'sandwich' them from above and below, and explore how these two pressures impact on their own pivotal relationships. They also need the agility to flex their own style, to ensure that connections are maintained throughout the organization. The following story illustrates how leaders, in wanting to protect their teams from the potentially destabilizing actions of their own leaders, can sometimes step in to 'absorb the shocks' but in so doing can create a greater distance between the layers of leadership at the very moment when connection is so critical.

CASE STUDY

We had been working with a COO who had asked us to support him as he reviewed his relationship with his CEO, and to help provide a neutral space in which he could explore some of his experiences of their relationship. From Michael's perspective it seemed that the CEO was very 'hands-off' when company performance was good and things were going well, but when there were problems he seemed to react with prescriptive tactics that had a direct impact on the activities of the divisions and did not appear to be well thought through. More often than not these tactics failed to address the problem and there would follow a detailed analysis of what had gone wrong. Another set of tactical actions would often follow.

Over time Michael became very conscious that he was protecting his own direct reports from the actions of the CEO, becoming a 'buffer' between the CEO and his own team and potentially 'drawing his fire' to enable his direct reports to continue their work uncluttered by tactical actions. When he stood back from the situation though, he realized that this 'protective stance' was inadvertently resulting in an increased distancing between the CEO and the department heads and leading to a greater level of frustration in the CEO. His attempts to provide an environment that would enable freedom of action below him was resulting in a greater dislocation between the top and the middle of the business. He started to explore how he could facilitate the dialogue between the CEO and his reports that would enable them to shift the patterns that were holding them all back.

This is illustrated in Figure 3.2. Taking on the buffer role can be meant as an act of good intent – a tactic often used in professional environments to protect the freedom of people to be innovative and creative at the very moment when this is needed. In mergers and acquisitions we have seen this strategy used to good effect to ensure that customer-facing teams are able to maintain sales performance and the continuity of the brand in the market, despite the changes being implemented within.

FIGURE 3.2   A 'buffer' between management levels

Business pressures on performance

Global CEO

Leadership buffer

Leadership team *with* space to act freely
but disconnected from strategic engagement

But it can also have an isolating effect, distancing less senior leaders from an appreciation of the pressures facing the business and denying the possibility of their engagement in co-creating ideas for action.

Questions you may find useful to consider here are:

- Are there times when you 'protect' your own teams?
- What impact does this have on their performance and motivation?
- When is protecting helpful? When does it hamper engagement and innovation?
- Are there more ways of involving them than you first think?

The 'go-between'

We see a related pattern of behaviour in this next story.

CASE STUDY

Christine had not been given the head of department role despite having previously led the team single-handedly, albeit with negative consequences for her personal life. She was surprised when a colleague whom she considered her junior was subsequently appointed to the role.

The relationship between the two had broken down following the appointment. Christine became withdrawn and spoke rarely to her new manager, instead focusing wholeheartedly on her work with her customers. The simmering conflict between the two began to impact their colleagues and one of them tentatively stepped into the role of mediator. He was supportive of both his colleagues and passionate about trying to get a resolution for the department, but his attempt at mediation seemed only to be accentuating the division between the other two.

The three colleagues had become trapped in the unspoken resentment and frustration of their disconnection and were failing to ask, 'How can we connect in a way that might be healthy and useful for each of us, and ultimately for our clients?' Their differences had just become too great and their positions too entrenched. These were polar opposites who needed to find a way of connecting, but by stepping into a mediator role their colleague had in fact failed to enable them to make the connection that was so critical to their recovery.

FIGURE 3.3   The 'Go-between'

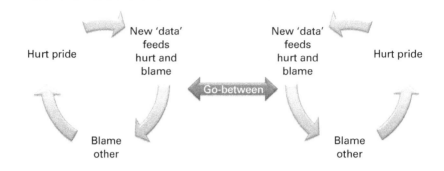

The pattern that can build up when a leader or member of a team tries to resolve differences without bringing the parties together is illustrated in Figure 3.3. In his attempt to smooth out the tension, the 'go-between' succeeds only in keeping the people involved in the dispute apart. Our experience of such situations tells us that resolution can only be achieved by enabling a dialogue in which each party is encouraged to see themselves through the eyes of the other. From here they can start to explore how they can gradually build a more constructive route to collaboration.

Bringing together polar opposites

If we are to value bringing in difference in an organization then we must similarly value the bringing together of that difference. To fully realize that value we must be able to 'hold the tension', creating a space in which we can both explore what that means for us and allow all the voices of difference to be heard. We see the strategic intent to bring in difference happening at all levels of leadership – and we see it succeed and fail in equal measures. In some cases the full commitment to making it work is just not there, and in others we suspect that the size of the gap is so immense that the difference is in fact unbridgeable.

Many leaders are familiar with the divisions that occur between different organizational factions: between geographies, functions, tops, middles and bottoms, and between key players who compete for status and power. We know that there can be enormous tensions in the 'system', many of them an integral part of the good health of the organization. They can help feed our curiosity and by using them to feed our inquiries can help catalyse new and exciting solutions. These can be heard embedded in the language of an organization, very often articulated as the conundrums or paradoxes that help define the operational norms. An example might be in the polarization of decision making, such as balancing the choice between a freedom to invest in high-risk innovation and a strict adherence to governance and cost control. One client working in a highly regulated section of the energy sector recently described the specific challenge as needing to explore how it might balance the need for compliance with the agility and pace that might enable it to define the future given the unpredictable challenges of climate change.

We have seen what can happen when we create 'buffer' roles. When seeking to connect difference it can also be tempting to be drawn into a form of dilemma resolution, yo-yoing from one polarity to another. Campbell and Groenbaek[3] refer to these as the A and B positions, and offer a methodology that helps co-create a middle, connecting place – the C position. As we worked with one client this was a useful framework to share as he sought to develop flexibility and variability on the one hand and governance and accountability on the other. We both knew that if we focused on one side we could potentially drive out the capacity for the other. We had already seen this happen else-where in the organization when one country head had focused so intently on building his operational basics that he had actually killed his organization's ability to innovate. Figure 3.4 illustrates how focusing on identifying the C position can offer up a much more positive outcome.

So, by holding each of the polarities lightly, and by focusing his attention on the coherent and connected opportunity they offered him, this client was able to build a team that could both work indepen-dently and hold itself mutually accountable to the organizational disciplines of targets, measurement and timelines. He recognized that he had to enable a local structure and culture that was highly adaptive, shifting the need for certainty from the traditional frameworks of process and role definitions to a coherence his team co-created at the

FIGURE 3.4   Bringing together polar opposites

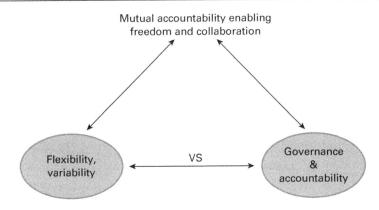

point of connection with their teams, with each other – and ultimately at the customer interface. He recognized that this fed an existing undercurrent of clashing cultures, and deliberately nurtured these connections to leverage the tension.

We've also seen this deliberate clash of cultures used as an effective growth strategy. In one case a global business deliberately put in place an outsourced model to provide the tension it needed to stay at the head of its market, co-promoting its products with a company that enjoyed a very different reputation from its own. It successfully co-constructed its new market position by connecting the 'cowboy' element of its partner's sales reputation with the 'science' of its own governance role. The success of the strategy was put down to co-leadership.

Another client has described how the company's founder had deliberately operated a 'Ying-Yang' management philosophy. He described him as going out of his way to build opposition, believing that by sustaining tension in the business he would drive compliance and effective governance. This required him to balance two polarities – total flexibility on the one side and friction and fall-out at the other. Each regional leader in turn dealt with the implicit tension and risk in the model. One regional head made this approach work by trans-lating it to work with his own style. He operated with a versatility that enabled all stakeholders to feel fully aligned. When the tension lost its constructive value he could easily diffuse it, combining a serious-ness and lightness in his style that could sustain the connection. It was only when this connection was broken by a United States-based executive introducing an inner and outer circle of leadership that the model began to collapse under the weight of unleveraged tension. Being forced to work separately and at arm's length severely weakened the touchpoints between them.

The following questions may give pause for thought:

- How many times do you frame your leadership conversations as polar opposites, in the form of either-or tensions?

- Where do perspectives and attitudes get exaggerated and polarized in your business?

- What opportunities can you identify to bring polarized positions together in constructive and respectful debate?

Deriving the best from difference in the boardroom

We can see the same challenges being created by the spectrum of difference in the boardroom. We know that the knowledge and experience to be able to challenge the CEO effectively are critical to successful governance but we also know that where non-executives are imported from a very different context it is very difficult to leverage their knowledge and/or experience base without an explicit determination to make it work. Although the appointment may appear strategically sound it can leave the board open to exposure. The same challenge can cascade throughout an organization, where deliberate difference is inserted (recruited) and then is rejected as the system fails to connect with the potential richness of the exchange. Soggy compromise is not a healthy option.

These roles and interrelationships at the top of public companies have been the subject of intense scrutiny, particularly following the banking crisis of 2008. Many questions were asked about the part played by key leaders in the failure of a number of leading banks, and how that might indicate the fundamental changes needed in the future governance and leadership of those businesses. Review committees specifically questioned whether the way in which boards were composed and run could enable a sufficient range of experience and perspective not only to be present but also to be allowed legitimate expression. They also raised questions about the ways boards were able to select and encourage the degree of contrasting knowledge and perspectives necessary to ensure that sound strategic decisions were made and risks objectively assessed.

In his review of corporate governance at UK banks and other financial entities, Sir David Walker[4] pointed to the importance of the chair in 'promoting an atmosphere in which different views are seen as constructive and encouraged,' noting that 'the pressure for conformity on boards can be strong, generating corresponding difficulty for an individual board member who wishes to challenge group thinking'.

Our own conversations with those undertaking non-executive board member positions indicate that this focus on conformity may well be slow to shift. On his appointment to the board in his first non-executive director position, one non-executive director commented that the rest of the board seemed far more concerned about his *fit* than in the different competence and perspective that he would bring to the debate. The other board members seemed to asking themselves whether they would get on with this new person rather than welcoming his competence and potential value.

Another non-executive director described his experience of trying to get the right balance in his contribution as 'trying to be integrated, aligned, resonant but also needing to be the grit in the oyster'. It's a graphic way of describing the need to hold onto the difference that is so valued at the point of recruitment.[5] Chairs clearly have to make fine judgements as they aim to appoint people who will play a strong and meaningful part in the board, who are able to confront issues that they see likely to put the business's future at risk, while at the same time respecting and aligning with the ongoing relationships and culture. Walker again points to the 'pivotal, wholly special position of the chair' in holding an effective relationship between the executives and the non-executive directors in leadership of the board, and emphasizes the need to encourage 'debate which is at the right point in the spectrum between unduly acquiescent and unduly intrusive'.

One chair of a European company has spoken to us about the importance of actively generating debate in the board room:

> *My predecessor didn't allow the employee representatives to have their say. He ignored them – but I believed that I couldn't afford to do that.*

Instead, I coach them on how to ask the right strategic questions. As a result they are being more constructive and more strategic in board meetings. This has the effect of them giving the board a more positive press in the organization. One of the challenges they made at the last meeting forced the management to go over their assumptions in the budget – which was helpful to the board itself.

Our own work with chairs and CEOs has underlined the pivotal nature not just of the roles but of the connecting relationship between these two office holders. This relationship creates the centre of gravity from which each steers and modulates the interactions and interrelationships between executive and non-executive directors. Where there is an incompatibility of style, or lack of shared mind, the fracture in their shared leadership can have an exponential impact on trust and teamwork across the senior leadership and throughout the business.

Again, there is a balance to be achieved. Walker points to the need for 'mutual understanding and respect' but says the two people should not be 'uncritically close', pointing to the need for trust and alignment, but also for the holding of distance and individual perspective. We saw first-hand how critical this ability to hold on to the distance could be when working with a CEO/chair relationship that was described as close and supportive by colleagues, but which at the same time had failed to attend to a situation in which the passionate and energetic interventions of the non-executive directors were greeted with resistance and accusations of intrusiveness by executive directors. More than one chair talked to us about the need for mutual respect, for adapting one's style to complement that of the CEO, and of the importance of humility in building a shared leadership relationship that goes beyond the sum of its parts and has a central role in building confidence and trust within the board so that difficult and challenging conversations can take place.

Recognizing the importance of the emotional connectivity between chair and CEO, we have invited some clients to be coached as pairs so that the dynamic of their relationship can be seen clearly played out in the room. In such situations, different perspectives on their respective roles, and emotional reactions to each other's interventions, can be interrupted, reflected back to them and subsequently seen in a new light.

Some of the relationship challenges that we have witnessed also highlight the potential for ambiguity in the respective roles of CEO and chair. While governance reviews have pointed to the importance of industry leadership experience in fulfilling a chair role, it is sometimes precisely this experience that makes it tough for the chair to stand back. Several chairs, who were executives in a previous life, have told us of the challenge and frustration they have felt in no longer having the remit to drive implementation, now having to 'sit on their hands'. One ex-CEO, now a chair, told us: 'I have to be careful about where I see the line. We now often have a conversation between us about where the line is.' Part of his role is in educating non-executive directors in how to conduct their own role: 'It is a case of remembering what hat you are wearing. Some board members link up with executive directors and forget their roles.' This chair's CEO affirmed the value that the chair brought in providing clarity about the roles and role boundaries on the board, and of using his executive experience constructively by providing strategic challenge based on experience and then standing back and supporting the CEO in his actions. 'He doesn't say, "I used to do it this way"...; he has high expectations, *and* he is hands-off... it is a relationship of mutual respect.'

Conversely, this CEO spoke of the difficulties he had encountered in the past when a certain board member had expressed a really strong desire to be CEO. His over-zealous need to drive execution both undermined the CEO's confidence and led to conflicting messages with his executive team. The CEO went on to say, 'specialist knowledge is very useful in a non-executive director, but what matters is the manner in which it is offered'. He mentioned the continuous balance that needs to be struck in ensuring that the non-executives were challenging enough, but not over 'prickly'. He found it helpful to pair up each board member with an executive, so that they could work together to develop mutually supportive roles and so that each saw the value in each other's contribution and perspective. One newly-appointed non-executive director in another company summed up the challenge this way: 'How do you know at what point you have fully expressed your difference and done your duty to shareholders?'

Igniting connective energy at the touchpoint

Creating connections that inspire others

Throughout our work with clients we focus on the growth of inter-dependent strength, facilitating insights into what will need to change to enable creative and interconnected dialogue and encouraging the need to value the points of connection. And we encourage them to remain curious where there is a feeling of being disconnected, alienated or trapped.

When asked what he thought made the greatest contribution to the success of his organization, one CEO answered unhesitatingly: 'Values trump everything.' When we pushed him a little further he explained that he saw his capacity to help liberate the energy of the individuals in his organization as critical to their collective ability to deliver the shared vision – and that this individual energy would be generated by the very personal motivations of each of them coming together at the touchpoint. He was able to track the changes in the quality of the energy he had experienced at the touchpoint as he had moved from one position to another. When we first worked with him he was struggling with the negative energy that was generated by his relationship with his CEO, oscillating between the optimism he felt for the proposition of the new company he'd helped establish and the sheer frustration and loss of confidence he felt when confronted by the CEO. We share his story to illustrate how the qualities of a single but pivotal relationship can be so disempowering, even for a senior leader, while at the same time that same leader can be so energized by the qualities of a pivotal relationship enjoyed with a fellow executive.

CASE STUDY

Separately both William and David were each inspiring and committed leaders – David was an entrepreneur and William a market specialist and key to the strategic growth of the company. But together they set up an action-reaction loop that sucked energy from the system and from those around them and left each of them feeling disempowered and angry. This friction led William to ask himself on numerous occasions, 'Does the CEO actually hear me?' Many times he doubted whether he could continue to invest his time and energy in the firm. He described how he felt mistrusted by David – in return becoming suspicious of the CEO's motives and actions. He felt watched, disempowered – and above all missed the close connection he expected from this critical relationship. But he believed deeply in the greater purpose of the business, felt personally connected to the endeavour, and relied on his passion to continually motivate others.

However, when we observed him working closely with another director colleague the positive energy and self-belief were extraordinary. They had worked together in a previous context, and had developed a mutually reinforcing relationship that derived its strength from their ability to continually feed the connection through patterns of exchange. It was this energy that helped him stay the course until he himself was appointed CEO and he stepped into a very liberated space. Since the appointment he has worked with this same colleague to co-create a sense of fun and energy that has clearly transcended the difficulties they each experienced under their previous CEO and they are now fully embedded in their new roles and taking their collective leadership to a new level.

When we met William again about 18 months into his new role we talked about the relationships that had proved significant in the journey, and those that were now holding him at his learning edge. He reflected on the great value he now derived from his relationship with his chairman. He described it as one of support, learning and trust. This relationship felt safe, and in turn had set the tone for a series of NED relationships that were similarly open and developmental, while maintaining a critical balance of governance and challenge.

He recognizes that he holds himself accountable to this question: 'Do I trust the person at the top to do the right thing by me?' He also holds trust at the core of his relationships, building opportunities to relate to individuals both within and on the edge of the business. Without trust he believes the exchange in the relationship is lost or, worse, it becomes false. In summing up the qualities of the relationships that have been critical to his success he names values and trust as core – which if breached catalyse the total breakdown of the connection.

The power of trust

One client found that this lack of trust was having a serious impact on his relationship with his global VP, with his energy swinging between extremes of positive and negative engagement.

CASE STUDY

Alan was a great sponsor of challenge and entrepreneurialism. His ability to trust his team and to encourage them to think 'out of the box' was core to his leadership philosophy. He believed in their capacity to become entrepreneurs within the global framework, and it was through his leadership that the UK operation had recovered its profitable position after several years of loss-making activity; on the back of that success he had been promoted to head up the European business. Not all the good ideas had paid off but as long as the managers learnt from the experiences Alan was prepared to invest in them again.

We had always been struck by Alan's ability to clearly articulate – and embody – his values. Whenever he talked through decisions, from making appointments to deciding whether to make changes in his leadership team, it was clear that loyalty, fairness and trust were high on his list. It was within this context that he shared his reflections after the first year in the new role.

He was struggling to find a way of connecting with his new boss. On the one hand he felt he lacked authenticity and found it difficult to really trust him; on the other he enjoyed the positive experiences of their intellectual connection, and referred to this as their most effective touchpoint. In this way they were able to co-create the level of energy necessary to establish a place of agreement and shared purpose. But by focusing on this intellectual connection he also saw much more clearly the lack of emotional connection in their relationship, and described it as less than whole. He had noticed a pattern emerging that kept them at arm's length and described his boss as drawing in the boundaries just at the point when they might have connected.

Alan also observed a similar pattern as this leader worked with the rest of his leadership team, and with some of the directors at the level below. He described him as connecting with the individual intellectual contributions they could make, while at the same time holding the team at an emotional distance. In his view this was causing it to fragment. Alan believed that the strong intellectual connections were actually feeding their separation and getting in the way of their collective ability to co-create a coherent and connected team.

FIGURE 3.5   The importance of trust at the top

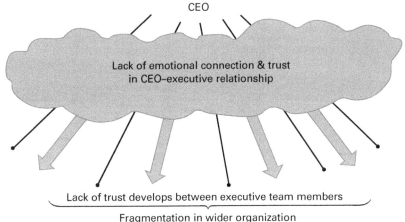

In this example we initially have an illustration of the positive energy generated by trust and emotional connection, and then see how easily that energy can be extinguished when the touchpoint is fractured. In this client's case we know that a subsequent culture survey, administered globally, indicated that senior leaders were perceived as not fully engaging people and even pushing blame down the organization. As their own energy was drained at the top through the loss of the touchpoint connection with their own leader, this leadership team triggered a ricochet effect right across the global company and in turn began to erode the trust of their own staff. This potentially debilitating pattern is shown in Figure 3.5.

The story illustrates how easy it is to allow a point of tension in the system to block the very dialogue and understanding necessary for change to happen. These blocks in turn very quickly become a reality right across the organization – the impact measured in levels of engagement, motivation and even creativity – and if left unchallenged can begin to unpick the value in the business. It's easy to become immune to this growing impact if current results appear to indicate success. The skill lies in remaining alert to those patterns of behaviour that disengage and demotivate, draining the energy out of the 'system' rather than replenishing it. It is remarkable how much this can be effected by the very individuals, teams and groups who themselves are adversely affected by it, their collusion evident in the repeating patterns but remaining outside their consciousness.

Liberating potential

We know from many examples that leaders have the capacity to liberate and ignite the energy in the system – and they have the power to extinguish it. Some connections can be hugely energizing, catalysing unforeseen changes to happen while others can become viral, slow-burn and even toxic. Without the right energy at the touchpoint[6] it is difficult to motivate, engage and develop others and over time the connections become more fixed and stuck and the energy ceases to flow. We might attempt to reignite it with a new programme launch or engagement activity but unless the energy is ignited at the touch-point of the pivotal relationships it is unlikely that momentum will endure. The skill lies in remaining alert to those patterns of behaviour that disengage and demotivate, draining the energy out of the 'system' rather than replenishing and growing it.

In the following example we show how two clients were able to focus on the tension that was threatening their capacity to create a collective leadership position and successfully redefined their relationship before it had begun to cascade to their teams.

CASE STUDY

When we first met Fiona we felt an immediate connection with her – she was vibrant, appeared full of confidence and determined to succeed in the new role. She'd been described to us by her MD, Lewis, as one of his brightest people; the issue he said was that she didn't fit. 'Fit' carries with it so many inferences, many of them relating to how we connect with difference, so we were initially wary about accepting the brief at face value. We suspected we might add greater value if we were able to explore ways of igniting the creative energy latent in that point of connection.

It was difficult to know in that first meeting what exactly Lewis meant by 'fit'. Fiona was certainly determined, had views on most aspects of the business, and was clear about her planned career trajectory. But it was difficult to pick up any insights into the relationship she had with Lewis. And of course we only had the one perspective – that of Lewis himself.

We invited the two of them to meet us together, expecting to review the scope of the work we might do, only to find that the meeting itself became the necessary work. As we watched them interact in the room we began to feel constrained by Lewis's tight hold on the direction of the conversation, and asked if we might offer an intervention.

We sensed that he was over-compensating for something he saw in Fiona and with which he wasn't comfortable. We also had a sense that he was apologizing for her while at the same time acknowledging that she was one of his 'best operators'. He wanted to encourage her to be less critical of others, to expect less of them, while at the same time relating to her in exactly the same way. She seemed barely there in the room, more an image in his story than a fully present member of his senior leadership team. As Lewis continued in this vein his behaviour visibly sapped the energy from her. She became trapped in his perception of her, devoid of any connecting energy.

We suggested a pause and encouraged Lewis to stand back and reflect on the conversation so far, to recognize the pattern that was locking the two of them into a less than helpful place. If Fiona was to step into a more resourceful, fully present place then Lewis would also need to help shift the dynamic between them.

In the following example we demonstrate how an individual leader can become trapped in his own patterns and inadvertently begin to extinguish the very energy he is aiming to ignite, actually diminishing the potential in some members of his team while apparently liberating the potential of others.

CASE STUDY

Jonathan had recently taken on the leadership of a specialist team and he'd been working on his individual leadership style. He appeared confident and articulate in his one-to-one sessions, although we didn't always feel connected to him, and we were curious to find out why this seemed so misaligned with the feedback we'd received from other leaders in the organization. They found him lacking in energy and drive, with low visibility across the group. We arranged to spend a half day with him as he met with his team for their monthly meeting. Our role was simply to observe and document what we saw.

We produced what we refer to as a 'map' of the meeting – the connections and disconnections, the creative highs and lows, the spectrum of contribution, the varying qualities of listening and energy flows. When we reviewed it with him it became clear that he was operating in two very different modes in the same meeting. He appeared to connect strongly with half of the group, listening attentively to their contributions and in many cases deferring to their views. When they spoke over the others he ignored it and ceded even more space to their discussion. The patterns were different when the other half attempted to speak. He appeared uninterested, interrupted them, cut them off short and appeared to encourage their colleagues to do the same.

Not surprisingly we had two very different qualities of energy in the room. The first group were confident, able to spark off each other, prepared to voice their difference and engage in healthy debate with the others. The second group appeared frustrated, spoke shrilly as they raced to finish their points and steadily raised their voices as the meeting progressed. There were no evident priorities for discussion and it was not clear if any decisions were made. When we left the meeting after around three hours the group appeared tired and seemed to have reached an impasse.

When we reviewed the verbatim text with him afterwards Jonathan was genuinely unaware of the effect he had had on the quality of interaction in the room and its catalytic impact on the nature of the energy he had helped generate. He was shocked to hear how transparent his judgement of his colleagues had been and how that had translated into the energy in the room. Probably most importantly he realized for the first time that he could make the difference between the team coming together as a connected and collaborative whole, sustained by positive and enabling energy at the touchpoint, and the team remaining fragmented, dysfunctional and frustrated by its own lack of power. We ask you to reflect: to what extent do you inspire others through the way in which you connect? Do you know whether there is potential you are missing by not fully trusting others?

Holding the relational space

Creating space for others at the touchpoint

We have already seen that trust is critical in helping build the touchpoint, and in Chapter 5 we illustrate how one leadership team invested time and energy in exploring how they could engender it both across the organization and in ways that would help connect it vertically. We worked with that client for nearly two years as they sought to transform their business in extraordinarily challenging circumstances. Several years later the CEO and most of his executives, hand-picked at the time, had moved on but three remained. These three had re-formed the leadership team, with one of them appointed CEO.

We reviewed the changes with them and questioned how they were managing to lead the same size organization with just three executives when the previous leadership team had been made up of eight or nine. We wondered how they were achieving the necessary bandwidth. They had a simple explanation for their success. First, by loosening their hold on the vision they had allowed staff to find ways of expressing their own passion for the work and no longer needed to put so much energy into motivating them. Second, by stepping back from the minutiae of operational control they had demonstrated such a level of trust in their next level of managers that they had immediately stepped into the vacant space, in turn allowing the executives to step back into their own.

We see this capacity to step out of the way – to enable others to step in and connect – time and time again, noticing a pattern of exchange and trust that leads to a positive impact on performance. We have seen some leaders challenged by this need to step back, their passion for the business driving them to take too much on themselves. One client played this out so clearly when we were working with him that we could actually see this action of stepping in and out as a significant shift in the touchpoint he generated with his team.

CASE STUDY

Stuart had previously asked us to work with him to help explore how he could bring a much deeper purpose to his corporate role and after several meetings had begun to find ways in which he could integrate a sense of his whole being without experiencing the familiar loss of energy that had previously undermined his progress. He was clear in his intent to 'help change the way this organization thinks about itself', a clear aspiration to work with the fundamental belief systems that kept the company trapped in its current persona.

He talked one day about his growing frustration with the limited success he was having in engaging his fellow executives. His own enthusiasm was evident. We invited him to map out his interaction with the team, representing each individual with whatever object came to hand in the room. We also asked him to represent himself. Although the selection of items can in itself have significance what mattered most here was the shape of the 'constellation'[7] he drew out, the physical and spatial representation of the underlying relationship structures offering valuable insights. He positioned his fellow executives in a broken circle, space left between them. He hesitated as he began to position himself, first putting his figure between two of the executives and then moving it to be placed between two others. When he finally settled on a position we asked what had been behind the movement. He explained that he was constantly on the move, trying to connect the pairs of individuals with his enthusiasm and drive.

We asked how that felt. Stuart shared a feeling of heavy responsibility, and remarked that each relationship was causing him hard work. He looked tired when he said it. We asked him to stand up and take a fresh look at the layout on the table. We invited him to walk around to the other side and see if he saw anything different from that perspective. After a few minutes' reflection he reached over and moved himself to the edge, alongside his colleagues. He visibly dropped his shoulders, sighed deeply – and smiled.

We asked him later what had shifted. His answer was quite simple: he had seen how the great effort he was making was paralysing his colleagues' capacity to act and relate. With all the best intentions he was actually getting in the way, standing between them as he tried to connect them. And so he decided in that moment to trust them – and stepped out. This in itself allowed him to step back in to a connective relationship with the team.

Through the constellation he recognized that he was taking a position that meant the others must relate in a 'hub and spoke' way, working with a belief that 'I have to drive them.' But when he saw clearly that he was in fact limiting and possibly even constraining their freedom to act and fully step into the roles, he shifted his belief to, 'They will do the right thing' and stepped back. By trusting them and taking up this new position he liberated each of them to take on new and powerful positions.

We experienced this need to 'step out to step in' ourselves when we worked with two teams of executives who were tasked with co-creating the next generation organization from an existing complex infrastructure of multiple bodies.

CASE STUDY

There were both current and future CEOs in the room, and a sub-set of their direct reports. In the one-to-one meetings we held as preparation for the work, we experienced mixed emotions as we heard frustration at the lack of pace and the existing leadership team's apparent reluctance to let go, and then a very clear shared purpose to help co-create something that would deliver the best service possible to a client who mattered deeply to them. With such a strong personal intent each was determined to influence the scope and outcome of the meeting.

In the first half of the day we encouraged the group to share their underlying beliefs and motivations for the work. Initially working in three sub-groups they developed a depth of mutual understanding and connection that they had not previously thought possible. There was still difference in the room, some of it teetering on tension, but they had successfully found a point of connection in their readiness to engage with the polarities they had explored together in their dialogues. The energy was tangibly high as we broke for lunch.

As we began to move on to action planning in the afternoon one of us took on the role of facilitator. After about 10 minutes we stopped the meeting. The energy had disappeared from the room. It felt as if we were dragging a huge boulder up an insurmountable cliff-face, and we said so. We stepped out of the facilitator role, joining them in the round, and offered a question to the group: 'What do you need to do now to re-connect with your collective energy?'

And the change happened. They stepped back into the connective behaviours they had demonstrated in the morning. New and surprising alliances emerged as a collective energy was released into the room even greater than the energy we had experienced in the morning. The two leadership teams appeared to change place. One of the 'new' leaders stood up and began to co-create the framework for the afternoon. The voices became louder. The current leaders seemed to let go and shifted from a driving role to a position of trust. Everyone began to give their input to the framework and it was clear that a value of mutual respect had been firmly established in the group. By the end of the day they had mapped out the whole of their year's plan, going far beyond their original expectation for the day.

What do we learn from this example? That there is as much value in stepping out as there is in stepping in – and that the art is in knowing when it is appropriate. Like Stuart we were trying too hard to engineer the very connection they needed to achieve for themselves, by working at their own touchpoint, and we needed to get out of their way.

So, we encourage you to ask these questions:

- How can I increase my influence for good in healthy, mutually beneficial ways and without getting in the way of others?
- How can I learn to affirm others in ways that are catalytic?

Growing mutual confidence

Many of our clients are challenging the traditional hierarchical models of power and authority and are questioning how they can lead with certainty just as the world is becoming increasingly uncertain and ambiguous. Research into stress has shown us that it is this need for certainty that debilitates, in some cases causing an obsessive focus on models of control that simply restrict the capacity to respond with creativity and innovation. So we constantly encourage those working with us to try a lighter touch, and to see the world through a systemic lens, discerning patterns that either help or hinder and learning to influence what emerges by paying attention to what really matters.

CASE STUDY

During one session with a client we were talking about the lack of institutional confidence in the organization, very much a product of the market environment of the last few years. He talked about the executive team (himself included) wanting to 'give confidence to the staff to start to lend again'. He drew a diagram on his pad, representing the staff as having created a shell around them that created a broad band of protection – and disconnection – between them and the clients. It looked like a sort of no-man's land, and it was becoming broader just as the business needed it to shrink.

If we stand back for a moment we can see clear parallel tracks here – in each case a reduction in resourcefulness as the individuals withdraw to a 'safe' place and inadvertently cut themselves off from the very energy they need to deal with the challenges. So we talked about confidence – and how any one of us might 'give' it to another. We wanted to help illustrate the dilemma and invited him to think about his different colleagues, reflecting on how each appeared to demonstrate confidence when challenges arose in the business. As he thought about it he drew up two columns, ascribing a different set of qualities to each column and then divided members of the team between them. He perceived one half of the group as needing to think everything through carefully, preparing and then acting. He recalled how some individuals in this group could become disheartened if things did not always happen as they had envisaged it would. They could even lose energy for the task. He described the other group very differently. They were much more 'gung-ho', full of energy for trying out something new and very ready to try again when it did not always work out as planned. We asked how he might envisage 'giving confidence' to each of these two groups, and he seemed very sure they would each decide for themselves when they were ready. The act of being confident was in their power.

It was an interesting exploration of confidence, but what was more important was the way in which he realized that these two groups also represented the two sides of the spectrum in the organization. On the one hand there were those who wanted to play it safe, get all the pieces on the board sorted before they stepped out into the ever-widening gulf between organization and client. They were expecting to create a touchpoint from a confident, expert place. On the other there were those who were ready to have a go, to step into what was inevitably a scary place but with the confidence of a learning pattern that would enable them to quickly recover their energy and focus.

We asked him to consider this question: 'How could you work with them to help build the confidence of these two groups – and the many versions in between – and ensure they're robust and sustainable?' As he thought about the proposition it became clear to Patrick that there must be a different way to look at the challenge. We talked about reconciling the two polar positions, and how he as a member of the executive team might embody the two ends of the spectrum as a way of creating space for that reconciliation. He had the opportunity to be the touchpoint – to help connect, to help liberate from an encroaching system of powerlessness, and by being the point of disruption in the system could also be the catalyst for a rich source of creativity and difference.

This then led to a conversation about the system that was holding them all in a potentially stuck place – the social system that currently sits in judgement on similar businesses in this sector, creating a whole series of touchpoints on the edge where the business needs to positively engage with the market and its clients. Instead they are holding themselves back from the edge, avoiding the risks – and remaining stuck in what they are probably mistakenly labelling a 'safe' but disconnected place.

Rather than seeing them explore the liberating patterns he knew the business needed, Patrick was seeing staff playing out his own debilitating pattern – their response to the negative touchpoints being the building of a protective barrier strip into which they wouldn't step. So, with reducing confidence they were reducing their operational space and therefore reducing their impact on the system... and so were unable to effect the very change that might start to resolve the situation.

Standing back to reflect on this leader it is clear that the executive team does recognize that there is an issue of confidence, but telling and cajoling is not having the required effect. Our proposition would be that they need to reframe the no man's land they've co-created and step into it as a highly energizing relational space. If the executive can lead the business to reshape these interfaces – to work at the touch-point that is causing them so much pain – then they might stand a chance of shifting the capacity not only of the business and the people on the inside but also those on the outside with whom they need to connect.

So the questions you might pose yourself could include:

- How can I hold my own sense-making lightly and begin to enjoy the ambiguity of our operating sphere?
- How can I co-create meaning from our difference?
- How can I ensure that it doesn't become fixed and exclusive?

We might even learn how to improvise, trusting each other to take the lead as each has a sense of their own relevant contribution.

Understanding the relational space

In the illustration that follows we worked with a team as it began to develop the insights and trust that would be critical to their capacity to do just this – to step out of the roles they habitually played and to step into the connective roles that the new organizational structure required from them. They needed to take on the co-leadership of a significant and Europe-wide transformation of the business through a new business partnering model that would require them to connect with themselves, their business leaders and the broader specialist community.

CASE STUDY

In his initial briefing to us the team's director, Thomas, had indicated that he was seeking an opportunity for the team to focus on its goals, explore how they might work best together to achieve them and begin to build some element of trust between them. It was also very important to him that the team get to know each other, personally as well as professionally, and that they leave the team coaching with development action.

We could feel 'gaps' in the circle but couldn't quite work out why. We shared with the group that we thought there was something we were probably missing and asked Thomas if he would trust us in the next exercise – which he did.

We asked him to step into the space at the back of the room – and it really was a big space, probably about 30 feet across and the same deep. He stood somewhere in the middle. We then invited each of the team to take up their positions in relation to him and in relation to their other colleagues. We asked them to do it without speaking and to move quite slowly, ensuring that they found a final position that truly represented how they currently experienced it.

Thomas found himself with just two of the team close by, with some very distinct cliques formed at quite a distance. One individual had placed himself at the other side of the room. One by one, and starting with Thomas, we asked how they saw their position, what they noticed about the people close by, what surprised them and how it felt to be in that position. Having worked with each one in the group we then asked each of them what it would take for them to take one step nearer towards Thomas. Where possible we invited them to action it in the room.

We hadn't intended to do this 'team sculpt' but it proved even more useful when they formed two groups to 'vision' what they might look like by the end of the year. They formed the two groups to intentionally close the gaps they'd experienced.

This team were particularly adept at holding each other at their learning edge, able to step into peer coaching roles whenever necessary and at the same time able to be both emotionally and intellectually present. We worked with them several times over 18 months and on each occasion they appeared to have grown in confidence and depth.

During one of their later workshops this same team had helped co-design a major activity centred on the key issues they'd identified during the earlier diagnostic phase. Having worked with them to help prioritize the list we invited them to try working with two different sub-groups, selecting colleagues from what they knew of their pro-files and preferences (some of this was derived from psychometric assessment data). Forming two concentric circles we invited one group to sit in the inner circle, with a spare chair, and then contracted for 'live action coaching'[8] based on what we'd observed so far, on the development goals they'd begun to set themselves, and on our own sense of what might be happening in terms of unhelpful patterns and behaviours.

We ran two fish-bowls like this, with time given partway through for reflection. Individuals shared what they'd experienced and observed, identified what needed to shift, made commitments to change certain behaviours, and then worked with the development goals in the second half. What was interesting was how much the group had learnt by the time they ran the second fish-bowl. Their capacity to listen was very different, they were bringing a new quality of attention to the debate, and invited views from others where they anticipated they would be different.

Building relationships as a connecting frame

By working with difference in this way – by holding it dialogically and appreciating the positive tension as a source of energy and insight – a connected but differentiated coherence begins to emerge. This dif-ferentiated coherence can unlock the action that otherwise becomes trapped by paradoxical choices and can open up the possibility of innovation occurring at the interlocking points. So, rather than viewing the paradox as a stark choice between two opposing options we can view it as the source of connective insight, engaging with each aspect of difference in a way that both affirms it and frees it up through the qualities of exchange.

We talked in Chapter 1 about the way in which the whole system begins to move under the momentum of just one of its parts moving. The organization becomes evident as an organic whole, able to move as if under implicit command as a critical decision is made in one part of the system, and through its connective threads the rest of the organization adjusts, realigns and co-defines its revised function and direction.

When a leadership team is working in a context of high ambiguity, where attempts to define coherence with any sense of permanence are likely to fail, this model becomes increasingly powerful as a means of understanding and adjusting the activities of leadership. When faced with enormous complexity in the business we can be tempted to seek order and coherence by attending to the framework of processes that appear to bind it together. Business process re-engineering and many of our total quality interventions have intended to do just that, and with high degrees of success. Order is established, uncertainty is minimized as the framework becomes the new certainty and the people operating the structure are able to liberate some of the energy of the organization from within these defining boundaries.

There are downsides, however. The energy that feeds creativity can become dissipated and constrained, the capacity for healthy challenge can become lost underneath the veneer of certainty, and boundaries that in their origins help define governance and safety become severely debilitating as the organization loses its muscles of courage and confidence.

We observed this first-hand when working with the transformational challenges of a highly complex business that was seeking to achieve a radical transformation of its structure over a very short period of time. Working with the CEO as he led the integration of two sub-units of the business to form one single entity gave us a very different insight into the challenges of holding coherence on the one hand and on the other enabling the organization to navigate the ambiguity. As the work progressed we began to see evidence that it was much more meaningful to use the term 'organization' to mean the people at the heart of the business and the way in which they connected or related rather than the more traditional references to corporate identity or structure.

We also saw evidence that it was in seeking to understand and articulate their work in this relational way that these networks of people were much more likely to sustain energy. They would also strengthen their capacity for timely decision making if they were able to embrace the constant re-forming of what they could depend on as 'certainty'. Within their volatile operating environment this 'certainty' would continue to shift and it would only be through their ability to hold each other in constructive relationship that they would be able to co-create coherent actions.

CASE STUDY

We first met the new executive team about three weeks after their appointment as an integrated leadership team. Their collective role was to lead the integration of the two businesses over an 18- to 24-month period, during which time they would also co-lead the formation and transition of a major part of the work to a series of new and separate enterprises. Some had previously held roles on either one of the previous two leadership teams, a couple were from related bodies, and two were leaders from specialist functions. These specialist leaders were to oversee the separate enterprises. They all either knew each other, or knew of each other, but in their telephone interviews with us prior to the workshop had highlighted getting to know each other as a priority.

The interviews had also highlighted that:

- individually they had a strong commitment to 'making it work';

- they recognized as a team that they needed to provide clarity and focus;

- they also recognized that they themselves had a high personal need for clarity and focus;

- there was a unanimous view that the focus on action and delivery was critical;

- collectively they had a strong drive to keep an 'outside in' view;

- they needed to balance a transition role with the provision of a sustainable future model.

These last two points gained increasing significance during the workshop and became their defining frame – the lens through which they viewed, explored and made sense of the challenges.

This was a team that understood the systemic nature of their role – leading the organization through the next 18 months of its life, attending to the needs of staff as they found themselves challenged by growing ambiguity, helping build a future legacy of which they might not even be part, and playing their part in delivering the change agenda. They were also able to be honest about the enormity of the task and articulated the extremes of the emotional swing as 'we're teetering around the edges a bit... we need to be radical' while at the same time admitting 'it's also quite scary'.

We had a day and a half for the workshop. This was quite a large team – 15, including the CEO and the two new specialist leaders. Two members of the team were unable to make the workshop so we had 13 in the room. It was important that they established the qualities of relationship that would enable them to work effectively together, so they spent the first couple of hours moving around the room in changing pairs, sharing their personal intent in contributing to the day and a half, being open about anything that might get in the way and committing to leaving it outside the door. They then invited the colleague in their pair to ask two things they'd like to know about them personally.

There was a level of scepticism clearly expressed in the room when we first introduced the activity, but this might have been because we framed the activity as 'speed-dating'! As they started to move around the room, changing partners every 10 minutes or so, they appeared to generate an energy as they found similar and dissimilar points of connection. It was hard to bring the focus back into the centre of the room at the end of the allotted time. When the conversations finally subsided we invited them to share what they'd learnt, been surprised by and newly appreciated about their colleagues. We were listening for the qualities of connection they'd generated.

One of the most noticeable shifts that had occurred was in the role the two future leaders were now playing in the team. Coming in from the outside it would have been hard to distinguish their contributions from the core members of the executive – a connection that was going to become significant in helping move the group forward later in the workshop.

They spent the rest of the afternoon in two groups, working on articulating the qualities of the relationship they both wanted and needed to build and sustain. It was in this relationship that they would need to locate the shifting power in the system, and it was through this relationship that they would need to deliver leadership to the system.

As the two groups came back together in the room and began to share the outcomes of their dialogues it was interesting to listen to the common language they were creating. They talked about developing a collective understanding, of liberating the potential of their staff, of ruthless focus, and above all becoming 'influencers by focusing on effective relationship management in the wider system'. These were their words. They also understood that being able to lead staff through unprecedented levels of ambiguity was going to be their biggest challenge.

We spent much of the second day focusing on the detail of how they would work together. This was built on four dimensions:

1 The unique contribution I can make.

2 The impact I will have on the system and the organization.

3 How we'll know I've succeeded.

4 How I need us to work collectively.

They spent just under an hour reflecting on their contributions and then drawing up their individual propositions on flipchart sheets. As the second part of the activity they each shared their perspective on their roles, building a collage across the length of one wall in the meeting room. As they listened to each other they began to develop a much deeper understanding of the collective capacity of the team, curious about their colleagues' deeper motivations for the work and challenging where they felt there might be omissions or overlap.

This created the opportunity for each member of the team to share their motivation, passion and special skill for the role before contracting with colleagues for the relationships they needed to enable them to deliver on their commitments. These relationships started to become very tangible in the room as they began to contract across their interdependencies. At the end of the session the CEO acknowledged the power of what they'd co-created and affirmed his confidence in the team when he said 'I realize I have an exceptional team'.

As they reflected on the session the team formed some significant clarity on its priorities, and increasingly focused its attention on how it might enable the staff to feel confidence despite the ambiguity. They acknowledged that they could only ever achieve a level of focus and certainty that would be transient and that roles alone would not give their teams sufficient framework. They began to talk about enabling them to better understand their contributions by helping them appreciate their value relative to the work of others, and relative to the current priorities. In this way they envisaged their staff understanding more about what they could deliver together, responding to the organizational needs in the here and now, rather than seeking to make sense of their contributions through prescribed role definitions. This way of working with and through the ambiguity would demand high levels of connectivity, the capacity to think in terms of personal and collective value and to be able to step over any false boundaries.

It was a new model for them, demanding that they provide absolute clarity on priorities and high-value work, and that they support their staff in learning what to *stop* doing. They knew it was going to be a tremendous challenge. They also knew it was the right model for this moment. The organization's capacity to connect, and the system's ability to move as one when just one aspect shifts, was going to be key to their leadership success.

Looking forward

We know that alongside our increasing need to make sense of complexity we have increased our need to define coherence, both personally and collectively. We are clear that this coherence must not be forced, and that any attempt to 'smooth over' the tension of difference will deny all parties their uniqueness, minimizing the capacity for innovation and leaving all parties bereft of a passionate attraction to the outcome. We each need to learn to stay with the tension and focus on the generative capability of the touchpoint. To do this we need to remain curious and able to engage in a dialogic way. So, our aim is to develop the capacity to hold together both separate and autonomous identities, engendering the affirmation of interdependent meaning that builds on our difference. We make sense of ourselves as human beings through our relationships and we grow as individuals as well as organizations. Our personal energy comes from this wholeness.

We are offering this view of leadership against a context in which the 'strong' leader has become attractive. In the previous section we proposed that we might redefine strong leaders as those who engender constant learning and thereby contribute to the long-term growth and sustainability of the business. Our proposition is based on our belief that it is the capacity to engender the essential touchpoints both laterally and vertically across the business that counts. And that the certainty of knowing that you are 'right' comes from your capacity to connect with and read your organization in ways that are resonant with both your personal and your collective values.

In the next chapter we explore what happens when we track the pivotal relationships that sit at the edge of the business, sharing examples of the challenges that arise when these connecting points become vital to the co-creation of value at the touchpoint with clients.

Notes

1 Bill Torbert and David Rooke developed a framework of seven action logics that can be found in Seven transformations of leadership, *Harvard Business Review*, April 2005. The authors draw on 25 years'

consulting experience and collaboration with psychologist Susanne Cook-Greuter to present a typology of leadership based on the way managers make sense of the world around them.

2 Joiner, W and Josephs, S (2007) *Leadership Agility: Five levels of mastery for anticipating and initiating change* (San Francisco, Jossey-Bass).

3 In their book *Taking Positions in the Organization*, David Campbell and Marianne Groenbaek (2006) set out a model of semantic polarities as a means of resolving instances where communication has become stuck in opposing certainties, or where truths have become entrenched or where one side is 'right' and the other 'wrong' (London, Karnac).

4 Sir David Walker presented his report, *Walker Report of Corporate Governance of UK Banking Industry*, in November 2009. The archived report can be accessed via the UK National Archive office at **http://webarchive.nationalarchives.gov.uk**.

5 See Thomson, P with Lloyd, T (2011) *Women and the New Business Leadership* (Basingstoke, Palgrave Macmillan). Thomson explores in some depth the issues connecting corporate governance and the banking crisis of 2007–8. Drawing on conversations with a cross-section of UK FTSE 100 chairmen and her work with senior women, she examines the possible dangers of 'groupthink' on board decision making and the potential value of increasing diversity in UK boards.

6 Bruch, H and Vogel, B (2011) *Fully Charged: How great leaders boost their organization's energy and ignite high performance* (Boston MA, Harvard Business Review Press). The authors build an energy matrix that illustrates four states of organizational energy, the goal being 'productive energy'. They have used an Organizational Energy Questionnaire (OEQ) to help measure and analyse a company's energy profile. The output is an OE Index that offers a picture of the four energy states, illustrating the degree of intensity and interplay among them. All four energy states are present simultaneously and so they offer a joined-up picture of the options. They then offer two strategies to help mobilize the organization's energy.

7 We use constellations as part of our coaching approach where the client needs to achieve an optimal working relationship, either individually or as part of a team. Our practice is based on the insights of Bert Hellinger, who developed the methodology as part of his work as a therapist, and on the work of John Whittington, who applies constellation practice as part of his consultancy work. See *Systemic Coaching and Constellations: An introduction to the principles, practices and applications* (Kogan Page, 2012).

8 'Live action coaching' is described by Mary Beth O'Neill as a way of the coach offering an unexpected yet useful intervention to help a client achieve their goal when they are in the process of conducting business activities and interactions. See *Executive Coaching with Backbone and Heart: A systems approach to engaging leaders with their challenges* (San Francisco, Jossey-Bass, 2007).

Transforming partnership through the touchpoint

The deep intimacy of our relationship is founded on the fact that we 'get' how our client's business works. It is built on trust and on behaviours that support the client organization's leadership of the change rather than simply driving a programme of change ourselves. **(LEADER IN A CONSULTING BUSINESS)**

Introduction

In this chapter we explore the value of applying Touchpoint Leadership principles within organizations whose success is dependent on supplying expert services to clients, drawing our illustrations from our development work with professionals who work at the client interface. Our experience tells us that the reputation of a services business is an amalgam of the ways in which it interacts with its current and potential customers and other stakeholders at the touchpoint of connection. The business brand comes alive through the relationships and the experiences that evolve between client-facing staff and their clients.

We bring first-hand experiences of how professional services firms have helped their leaders develop the skills to bring their expertise and perspectives to the client interface in a way that creates deep understanding of and connection with the client's needs and wants. We explore what this means for the relational capacities of client-facing staff and how personal development can enable them to 'prime' this type of relationship touchpoint. We give illustrations of where bringing the 'whole self' to the touchpoint has enabled professionals to enhance their capacity to work creatively and productively at their learning edge with clients, and to be accepted as a trusted adviser, while reaping benefits for their own overall sense of life purpose.

We also look at the challenges faced by services businesses as they strive to optimize the value of touchpoint connections across their own internal divisions. The creation of coherence and collaboration across functional expertise, service type, sector focus and geography is essential for them to provide integrated services that attend to the increased complexity of the client organizations they serve. We look at how partnership governance structures, developed to enable shared ownership, can often engender a degree of competitiveness that disrupts partnering behaviours within the business, potentially hampering the firm's ability to create integration and coherence at its connecting points with the client system.

Finally, recognizing the growth of the internal partnering relationship model over the past two decades, we point to the relevance of this learning to internal client-partner relationships, signposting to Chapter 5 where we look more closely at the value of liberating potential through attending to the touchpoints that will in turn co-create the collaborative enterprise.

The professional partnership 'brand in action'

Today's global professional service organizations, comprising, amongst others, accountants, consultants, lawyers, financial advisers and engineers, face a constant challenge in differentiating their services from their competitors and thus 'standing out' to secure and grow their place in the market. The range and quality of their services, their expertise, their sources of technology and the innovation in their thought-leadership are all critical to their differentiation, and therefore the quality of people they recruit, their dedication to professional development and standards, and their access to innovative learning opportunities are key to business success.

Most firms of this nature have long realized that their means of differentiation lies not purely in their product and service range, but in their ability to adapt to the scale and specific needs of their clients. Therefore the quality and nature of the relationships they build with their clients is critical to their competitive success. Indeed, with the explosive increase in the flow of information and know-how in recent years and the consequent challenge of providing a substantive innovative competitive edge in many services, relationship has become the *prime* source of differentiation. As a consequence, many professional services firms have made substantive investment in programmes that enable client-facing professionals to acquire and build the skills through which they can foster and grow such relationships, in the knowledge that, when taken as a whole, these relationships – and the touchpoint moments within them – add up to the aura and image of the firm and become, in essence, its 'brand in action' or 'living brand'.[1]

For many highly skilled professionals, the need to hone their social skills, to devote time to the nuance of the relationship as well as to the excellence of the product or service, can pose a significant development challenge. Those who are most effective, however, recognize that this is a vital learning step if they are to expand their ways of relating effectively with clients, represent the breadth of services that the firm can provide, and differentiate the nature of those services through the relationship process. Our own experience tells us that these challenges continue to persist within the industry despite considerable attention to, and investment in, this area in recent years.

Transformation of a professional partnership firm's 'brand in action' needs, in addition, to go well beyond a change in the individual-client relationship experience: it requires systemic coherence, across a governance model that was originally designed to give contributing partners a degree of freedom to develop and practise their professional expertise while holding a stake in the business, where a partner's remuneration historically reflected his or her personal revenue performance. Such a governance model places prime value on nurturing professional accountability and growth in the interests of innovation, client service, and brand differentiation.

The increased scale of partnership firms over the past 20 years, fuelled by the drive to create businesses with multiple service offerings, serving ever more globally integrated client businesses has, however, placed significant pressures on the partnership governance model. Leaders of such businesses face the challenges of drawing on the best expertise from different sources of know-how and experience to provide a seamless service to an individual client business; of creating a culture and system that fosters individual excellence and attainment while also providing a team-based service in increasingly complex and geographically spread projects; of allowing freedom of operation to highly skilled people while ensuring the accountability and control necessary for business success. Creating a compelling and competitive global 'brand in action' therefore requires attention to the complex interplay between geographically spread, multi-layered, multi-person systems of client and service provider, and demands as much focus on the internal relationship touchpoints of the services firm as those that face the client directly. As a consequence many partnerships have changed their performance management and remuneration practices in an attempt to encourage more collaborative working between individual partners and between geographical locations.

Here we explore the different dimensions of 'touchpoint' that need to be addressed at the personal, inter-personal and cross business level – our 'three-tiered connectivity' – for a business to truly differentiate through relationship. We start with the opportunities that exist for client-facing leaders aiming to transform their impact with clients, and therefore their embodiment of the firm's brand, in a way that builds increased value for both the client and the firm. We then move on to the challenge of creating touchpoints within complex service businesses.

Bringing a new sense of self to the client interface

CASE STUDY

Chris was a consultancy partner who spent most of his time with clients. While he was a highly successful partner commercially, he was seen within the partnership to need to develop more positive relationships with his peers and this was hampering his promotion. He had been told that if he failed to develop his internal partnering presence he would not advance, regardless of his success with clients. This he felt was unreasonable given his commercial success and the quality of his relationships with clients. It was unclear to him what he needed to do to meet the demands of the firm.

At our first meeting Chris was excited – he had been invited to meet the CEO of a global pharmaceutical business to discuss its business strategy. He had been recommended for this meeting on the basis of other work that he had done in this area and the CEO wanted to talk to him about doing similar work with his senior team. Chris was anxious for this meeting to be a success and was mulling over how he would best introduce himself, how he should assert his authority and what connection he could make to get the meeting off to a good start. He thought that a good approach would be to remind the CEO that he, Chris, had done a project for him some years back when he was a consultant – it had gone rather well and the CEO (in the role he had at the time) had said so. By referring back to this positive time in the past, Chris thought he would make a good point of contact.

Or would he? As Chris started to reflect on this he came to realize that, despite the fact that he had been asked by the global CEO of a leading business to go to talk to him about his strategy, he was planning to legitimize his presence with the past achievements of a junior consultant. He realized that he was at risk of entering the room linked to an image of himself that was potentially no longer valuable, and which might hinder his acceptance as a strategic partner who was entitled to converse as an equal with the CEO of a major global business.

Of course we never found out what the impact would have been if Chris had greeted the CEO with, 'You probably remember me. I supervised a project for you back in 1990 – I remember you were very pleased with it.' But our assumption is that Chris would have presented himself as a bright but subservient junior to an 'important man', rather than a potential equal, and that his strategy conversation would have flowed less well than it did. He would have created an initial touchpoint that set the scene for the conversation that followed, influenced by his assumptions and beliefs about his role and contribution as a consultant whose self-worth was only as good as his successful projects, rather than a fellow business professional who deserved to be there and whose company the CEO would value.

We encourage you, as reader, to consider whether you have ever put yourself – consciously or unconsciously – into the position of a 'junior', and, if so, what were the consequences, both immediate and longer term? As for Chris, he started to see, over a period of time, that many of the interactions that he had with people were based on a transaction – an exchange of advice or courtesy – rather than a relationship of equals that had meaning and value that went beyond the product or service being discussed.

That clients look to professional services firms to provide knowledge and experience that they themselves lack is beyond dispute. What intrigues us is the extent to which professionals respond to this need by believing that such experience is the only or prime source of legitimacy, and that their personal value is determined by the extent of their having superior technical knowledge and skill. In his book-*Managing the Professional Services Firm*, David Maister describes the typical professional as someone who is 'driven to seek out the new', who values autonomy to develop expertise and achieve personal goals and whose need to be recognized is accompanied by a personal sense of insecurity, a 'low sense of self-worth'. Such a person's self-belief is often nourished by focusing on 'unambiguous' challenges and by developing superior skills and knowledge for use with clients.[2] Engagement in broader conversations in order to build rapport and deepen relationships can feel uncomfortable and be labelled as peripheral – even a hindrance – to the core advisory role.[3] As well as having an impact on client relationship building, the professional's need for personal achievement and recognition can hinder his or her willingness to collaborate and thus to integrate different services and skills in a way that makes sense to a business client. For this reason, a number of professional services firms have drawn on the fields of adult learning and behavioural change to help their highly skilled professionals build more relational sources of legitimacy, within the firm and with clients.

As consulting firms have sought to have more strategic and transformational impact on their client organizations through the delivery of complex change programmes, many have focused development initiatives on their most senior client-facing staff and their ability to engage with executive and board-level clients in relationships that will last long term. One such consulting business recognized that the key to creating more value in the way consulting services were sold and delivered lay in a shift in the relationship between the buyer of the service and the seller, but there was ambiguity in how this could be brought about.

CASE STUDY

The firm commissioned an inquiry aimed at getting insights into the attitudes, needs and experiences of the 30 CEOs and executives of major businesses, and also the views of 30 role model client-facing partners as to what it would demand of them to work with this level of client, in both a selling and delivery capacity.

The inquiry with the partners uncovered some assumptions and beliefs that we have since seen in other professional services firms. The first was the general feeling that the 'C Suite' or board presented new and significant challenges for them, requiring a far greater breadth of business acumen and more gravitas than was felt to be needed when consulting at functional head level. Secondly, it was assumed that the 'solution' to the skills gap would lie in a report of recommendations and a teachable set of approaches, know-how and tools that partners would be able to adopt and learn to build their board-level consulting capability – perhaps not a surprising expectation in a culture that valued applying expert judgement to the solving of problems.

The results of the inquiry into clients' views, however, demonstrated that the shift needed of partners went beyond a set of tools and techniques. CEOs and senior executives saw the technical expertise that their consulting advisers brought as a 'given'. If partners were to differentiate themselves as 'board level' consultants, CEOs were looking for a business partner who was, first and foremost, interested in them and their business, and able to focus and adapt his or her conversation to meet their needs: the presentation of consulting methods through pre-prepared 'decks' was of little concern to them. They admired consulting partners who were authentic in their behaviour, who showed interest in them and real passion for their business. They also expected challenge and innovation, an ability to talk about a wide range of business topics and to provide a perspective borne from experience in other businesses and sectors. In other words they wanted someone with whom they could have a relationship of equals, who would be a confidante and sounding board. Linking to the work on leadership of Bill Torbert,[4] clients were setting a challenge to their advisers to move beyond a form of 'client leadership' that was 'expert' or 'technician' level to one that embraced elements of the diplomat and strategist level leader.

Feedback of this type can be surprising and uncomfortable to professionals whose success to date has been founded on the development and application of deep knowledge and skill. We have encountered many professional advisers who cannot imagine being in a situation where they do not have a methodology or piece of 'thought-ware' to explain, present and sell. As one partner has told us, 'I cannot believe that any client would want to spend time with me if I did not have a technical solution to give them.' This sentiment is increasingly outdated as purely technical services become more and more commoditized. Some professionals, however, still experience a genuine fear of being caught in a conversation where they do not know the answer, or of moving from an 'expert' to a more personal or business agenda. This fear has been prevalent since the financial crisis of 2008 when many firms have been forced to look beyond their traditional client base and build new relationships with unfamiliar businesses and in new territories. Like Chris earlier in this chapter, such professionals can look up to clients at this level in an intimidated and inferior way, and lack the belief that they can meet executives as equals in the executive suite or board room. When this anxiety is carried into the executive meeting, clients quickly sense it. Some have told us that consultants can be 'arrogant without being confident' – a phenomenon that can arise from the overemphasizing of superior knowledge in an effort to conceal felt vulnerability. This can clearly lead to a tangible disconnect with a client who is looking for authenticity and support.

Creating a learning vehicle to enable new ways of connecting with clients

In the case of the consultancy described above, designing a set of interventions to enable the senior partners to take in the feedback from the client inquiry and to start to explore what it meant for them personally posed a conundrum. In a culture where expertise is valued, people, especially successful ones, do not like to admit to not knowing, to being unsure of themselves or to making mistakes. Expertise and excellence can be seen as 'getting it right', rather than being 'constantly in a learning place'. Partners were seen to be the people in the organization who had undertaken personal development to their current level but who had now 'made it to the top'. And yet to become trusted through the type of relationship that their clients wanted, these partners had to be prepared to unlearn, to deal with ambiguity and to be prepared to show vulnerability – a quality fundamental to Touchpoint Leadership. The learning process would need to go far beyond a set of consulting methods: it would need to engage each individual in a process of personal growth so they could each find their own unique way of bringing to life the new type of relationship partners that their business strategy required. For a highly successful person to break well-honed patterns of response and conversation can be disorientating, even disturbing. The business started to realize that it was inviting some its most valued senior business people to make a shift not only in their behaviour but also in their beliefs about themselves, their work and about their interrelationships with clients.

CASE STUDY

So how did this organization help its partners to unlearn some of their behaviour and learn new behaviour in order to bring a new type of partnering presence to their touchpoint with clients?

First, the business needed to appeal to the partners' personal criteria for success, by reinforcing the commercial and personal gain to be achieved from changing. The personal shift required was linked firmly to consulting work of the highest status and value in the firm – there was a strong incentive in being successful in this area.

Second, because of the personal challenge this presented to the partners involved, it was important that the learning approach was seen to have commercial validity. The most important 'selling point' for partners' development was that being flexible in one's ways of interacting helped one build productive relationships more quickly. The business knew – and it was reinforced by client feedback – that it was unusual ever to be given more than 30 minutes with a chief executive. Partners started to realize that through enhancing their ability to relate well with clients, they could get to the heart of the issue in a one-to-one conversation more quickly. Where previously they might converse about the task or project and then, separately, either before or afterwards, enquire about the client's family or spare-time interests, now they could conduct a conversation that enabled them to attend to a client's personal issues within the context of their business challenges. They learnt that as their clients became more comfortable talking to them personally they would be more willing to share the challenges in their role and for the company as a whole. They were then able to start using more powerful questions in their dialogue with their clients, such as: What are you hoping for personally from addressing this challenge? What concerns you most – keeps you awake at night? What gives you most pride and a sense of satisfaction? What are your hopes for the next five years, for the company, your own career, your family? What is the legacy you would like to leave behind you? These questions helped partner and client engage in a conversation that had more value and relevance to both parties and facilitated deeper connection and collaborative learning between them.

Third, the development challenge needed to be real for each person. Each partner was provided 360-degree feedback data from clients and colleagues and face-to-face developmental feedback focused on areas outside their professional knowledge or competence. Through this each individual received data they could not ignore if they were to continue to be successful.

Fourth, it was critical for the business to create an environment in which people felt able to be open about their development areas, their uncertainties, and in which they would be prepared to try some new ways of behaving. This was partly about safety – about not feeling foolish in front of others – but it was also about business legitimacy, that the time invested was clearly linked to the day-to-day business in which they were involved. This was addressed by designing a development intervention in which learning groups of four to six partners enabled participants to bring their own real client relationship issues to be explored and addressed in the group.

It was essential that, having invited partners to share their client challenges with their colleagues, they were not allowed to offer each other solutions. That would have reinforced the 'expert' consultant behaviour with which they were familiar. Instead, each partner was required to coach another in their group in how to address their client relationship challenge. To help the 'partner-coach' to expand their ways of helping, we introduced them to John Heron's model of intervention styles.[5] This model distinguishes between those interventions that a 'partner' makes where he or she believes instinctively that he or she has the know-how to help the client (the authoritative interventions) and those where the partner feels that his or her role is best served if he or she intervenes to release the know-how that is already within the client (the facilitative interventions). Application of this model helped partners recognize tangible value in those aspects of dialogue that were not habitual to them, and to help expand their range of ways of relating at the touchpoint of their connection with the client.

The objective was for the partner to create a relationship environment with the partner 'coachee' in which the coachee was helped to address his or her challenge without the 'coach' solving his or her problem for them. The partner 'coach' was therefore learning and practising skills that he or she could use when conversing with his or her C Suite clients.[6,7]

Table 4.1 illustrates the range of responses to a 'typical' client situation that could be made, using John Heron's six intervention styles

TABLE 4.1 Using John Heron's Model of Intervention styles to expand the conversational range

Example comment from client: 'I have become concerned about the performance of my CFO'	
Name of Heron Intervention style	Potential response from partner
Prescriptive (Provides direction):	'You need to start talking to head hunters'
Informative (Provides information):	'In my experience it is normal for new CFOs to take a few months to settle in'
Confrontative (Provides new insight):	'You have been saying that for months and you haven't acted on your concerns'
Catalytic (Helps new understanding):	'Tell me what you are most worried about. When did you notice this? What else concerns you?'
Supportive (Provides greater sense of self-worth):	'You have done everything you can to deal with this problem.' 'What can I do to help?'
Cathartic (Enables release of emotion):	'That must be very disappointing for you.' 'If you were to voice your frustration fully what would that sound like?'

framework, and illustrates how application of the model can help someone expand their range of responses to one potential comment from a senior client.

The consultancy was not telling its partners that solving problems was wrong – rather the reverse. It was saying that if a partner had only one way of responding to a statement from a client, this limited the creative climate for exploring more diverse and innovative approaches to the client's issues and problems and restricted the range of clients with whom he or she could build rapport. Also, if a partner were to be a strategic adviser and coach, he or she would inevitably be having conversations about issues that were outside of his or her knowledge: It was critical to be able to handle ambiguity in conversations without loss of authority and presence.

Developing the confidence to be vulnerable at the touchpoint

The different ways in which we as human beings access and exert our personal power in relationships is well summarized by Hawkins and Smith.[8] The authors distinguish between power based on what you know and what you have done (your authority), how well you relate to others, especially in the moment (your presence), and your ability to shift the energy between people in the room – both intellectual and emotional (your impact). The ability to use all three sources of power, they argue, is critical in building leadership and partnership influence. Hanafin and Tolbert[9] take a related approach, distinguishing between three different aspects of presence – past presence (akin to Hawkins' authority); present presence (how one 'turns up'), and future presence (like Hawkins' impact), the ability to create shift in the moment, but also the ability to bring the future into the room, through hope, aspiration and creating an impression that lasts. The source of personal power accessed by the partners in this case study – as in many highly qualified professionals – was most often 'authority' or 'past presence'. Expanding their ability to relate and to generate change with clients required them to develop a greater ability to access power in the other two dimensions – present and future presence. Through building their ability to be confidently present and open to whatever was arising in the client conversation, the partners were opening up ways in which client and partner could create new thinking together, thus providing the opportunity for collaborative strategic partnership.

Table 4.2 summarizes the nature of the shift that these partners started so as to create a more relational touchpoint with their clients[10]. The table shows that changing the nature of partner-client interactions from those where providing expert solutions was the prime model of

TABLE 4.2   Transforming the brand at the relationship touchpoint (built on Hawkins and Smith)

The relational capacity of the partner	Moving from:	To embrace:
Ways of conversing	I use one or two familiar ways of intervening to establish technical expertise	I consciously draw, from a range of interventions, the one which will best help the client now
	I control the conversation within safe boundaries of my specialism	I am willing to engage in conversation on a range of subjects, including those where I lack superior knowledge or expertise
Engagement of feelings and emotions	I see the client's feelings as separate from the work conversation and secondary or irrelevant to the professional partner–client conversation. I tend to avoid them	I see the client's feelings to be legitimate and central to the dialogue. Failure to attend to them stops me helping the client and their organization and curbs my impact and influence. Skillfully sharing my own feelings can also help the client
Personal belief, identity and mindset	My sense of self and self-confidence rests on my ability to give technical advice: I am only OK if I know an answer	I am OK about not knowing: this does not impact on my self-confidence: listening is often a valuable intervention in itself
	My role is to provide expertise in a rational detached manner	I have a legitimate role in challenging my client's thinking and behaviour
	A meeting is a step in a sales transaction I am here to solve your problem	A meeting is part of a growing relationship, which may have a mutually profitable outcome I am here to partner with you and together look for new directions and approaches
	I am junior to you/I am senior to you and know better than you	I am a business peer

delivery to those that involved open-ended, dialogic, exploratory, broad-ranging dialogue, required the partner to change more than just their actions and behaviours: It required them to bring more of themselves into the room, to be more open to emotions – those of the client and their own – and this meant being more alert to what was *not* being said as well as what *was* being said; and it needed them to be able to embrace new beliefs about their own value in the interaction and their role as a business adviser. From this place of stronger legitimacy the partner was able to give deeper and more authentic support – and also more robust challenge to his or her clients, where he or she saw a client's behaviour to be out of step with the interests of their business. The partners were bringing more of themselves and relating to their clients more fully as human beings, rather than as people to be advised or sold to. They were developing the capacities of full presence and mutual learning that we describe in Chapter 2 in order to *prime* the touchpoint of their relationship.

Figure 4.1 shows diagrammatically the developmental process through which individuals can develop greater authenticity in their business relationships, when one person in a relationship pays attention to the other's needs, hopes, emotions and beliefs, and also stays tuned to the responses that spring up in them – the knee-jerk reactions, the feelings, the empathetic responses. Being aware of this 'data' provides the partner with more choice as to how to respond to the other and to generate new knowing in collaboration with them. This awareness is complemented by having the ability to stand back from the situation overall and to tune into the dynamics in the business context that may be impacting on the interpersonal touchpoint of connection. These three main forms of awareness are the foundation level of Figure 4.1.[11]

The second level of development is that of enhancing the repertoire of interventions and responses that can be applied to any interaction. Mastering the ability to unlock the greatest value for the client requires astute attention to what is happening in any moment and an ability to manage one's automatic responses – a key ability of 'Touchpoint Domain 2', as described in Chapter 1. This means being prepared to stay grounded regardless of what 'comes up' – an ability

FIGURE 4.1   Building greater openness and authenticity in relationships through being more vulnerable

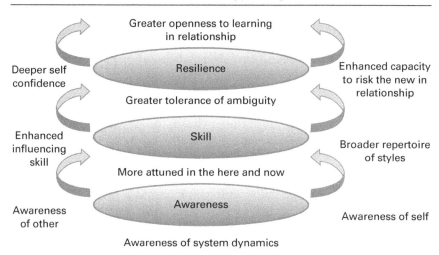

to tolerate the unknown rather than seek to affect the outcome with prescription or control. Thus the partner is increasing his or her preparedness to take risk – to be vulnerable – in relationship, a quality that is the essence of authenticity – and to deeper self-belief. As one of the consulting practice leaders who participated in this development programme stated:

> *I learnt that if you are disposed to react in certain ways to things,*
> *people, events – it is best to create a distance between your reaction and*
> *what you do about it. This gives you choice in what you do and say.*
> *It doesn't slow you down; it makes you more alive to what is going on.*

The value of being alert to one's own feelings and reactions in response to another's was well illustrated by a partner who went one day to interview a senior programme leader about a programme of work within his business that needed consulting support. During the conversation in which the client described the type of support that was needed, the partner was struck by an overwhelming sense of boredom and pessimism about the work being described, despite the fact that, on the face of it, this sounded like a very challenging business change programme. He knew that unless the conversation shifted, he would be unable to feel inspired to develop a proposal of work that would help this potential client; that he would not be able to help the client unless he shared his experience of being bored. When he did so, the energy of the programme leader seemed to be unlocked: he started openly sharing his worries and concerns about the programme, and the partner was able to explore how he thought he could help.

This partner took the risk to be as different from the potential client as he could by giving voice to the emotions that were blocking his creativity – something that up to that point the client had been unable to do – while at the same time finding a way of connecting emotionally and empathically with him to build a space for creative conversation.

The art, practised by a consultant, of holding difference in a dynamic way while connecting empathically is well described by Nevis in relation to organization consulting:

> *The practitioner is generally more open and revealing about the thoughts and feelings than might be true in other forms of process consultation. The aim is to take advantage of the issues of difference, marginality, and attraction by the client so as to use oneself in the most powerful way possible.*[12]

By starting to have different types of conversations with clients and by bringing a new sense of themselves into their client interactions, these partners were able to start building relationships in different ways – relationships that were more highly valued by clients and more rewarding for the partners concerned. They were able to shift the touchpoint of their interaction with clients away from a dominance of sharing expertise and knowledge transfer to one where the relationship generated new 'knowing' in a co-creative, generative way. A key requirement for a deepening relationship was the capacity of the partners to bring more of themselves to the touchpoint and to be at their learning edge in the moment of interaction, as described in Chapter 2. In building the willingness to risk not knowing in the presence of a senior client, these partners were able to find a new sense of confidence in themselves – fewer situations fazed them because they knew they would have the resources to handle them. As one partner said, 'The main thing I have learnt is to be able to say that I don't know the answer, with confidence.'

In bringing more of their whole selves to the touchpoint they were also encouraging their clients to be more 'whole'[13] and therefore more invested in their work and its meaning for themselves and their wider life. And they were also building partnership relationships that endured. A return on investment (ROI) study conducted two years after the start of the programme, showed a significant increase in business developed by those partners who had participated in the programme. This change had come about by attending to how they responded at critical moments – or touchpoints – in conversations.

Consulting partner stories

I had arranged to see a CEO of a major bank and felt exposed because I had not had time to get properly briefed. I decided my only choice was to listen – anyway, this is what the programme had suggested I do. So I listened to the CEO's worries and concerns... and that was the start of a very strong relationship with that client.

Until I went on the programme I believed my role was to criticize clients. I have now started praising them too – it has made a big difference to my relationships.

Clients always told us they wanted more challenge, but I didn't think they really meant it. I found a way of being bolder – holding up the mirror to their behaviour. I was able to do this in a way that showed I really cared about their business. The relationship became far more productive and enjoyable from that point.

What these quotes in part illustrate is the increase in the humanity of the interaction between consultant and client. The partners were putting more of themselves into the interaction, and therefore putting themselves at risk, and were allowing their clients to be more themselves. Thus they were starting to build relationships that would enable more transformative conversations at the personal and the systems level of change. The way they started to see and conduct themselves in relation to clients is illustrated in Table 4.3.

TABLE 4.3   Building Touchpoint Leadership capacity to build and deliver client service – core elements

Intrapersonal coherence
Knowledge and expertise – bringing the truth + presence, not knowing, being vulnerable
Sense of self based on what I know + sense of self based on who I am
Interpersonal coherence
Serving, deferential + equal partner
Confident in self and contribution + humble, adaptable, giving credit to others
My expertise and depth of knowledge + our collective, evolving creativity
Matching + bringing contrast
My difference + our empathic connection
Organizational coherence
Consistent and coherent brand image + adaptable, alive, spontaneous image
Our collective brand + my personal brand

Building a coherent client relationship through connecting internal touchpoints

While transforming the touchpoint of the partner-client interaction is a critical element in changing the nature of the professional service as experienced by the client, that client experience is created by much more than one-to-one interactions: it is dependent on the alignment of individuals often engaged in the different teams with contrasting and complementary specializations. As mentioned at the start of this chapter, in professional service teams who serve global client businesses the interrelationships are often diffuse and complex, but to the client business that they serve they need to appear seamless. Ensuring not just alignment but also the fostering of innovation and productivity across these interconnections is a critical source of competitive advantage. As one executive team member of a global company told us: 'I need my advisers to be more joined up than we are. But they are often less joined up – so they cannot help us in the way we need.'

So client-facing partners in a global firm need not only to attend to and develop the most effective relationships within their client organizations, they also need to orchestrate a labyrinth of interconnections within their own business, connecting client knowledge and insight with sector expertise, process methodology and technology, often across multiple teams in multiple geographies. A failure to orchestrate the touchpoints across these boundaries can not only lead to sub-optimal use of highly trained resources, it can make the partner-client relationship vulnerable, and endanger the broader reputation of the firm.

As we stated earlier, the unique cultural and motivational characteristics of highly professional environments can make building such creative cross connections particularly challenging – a phenomenon that is experienced in other sectors where professional expertise is a source of competitive advantage such as the pharmaceutical, engineering and, in the public sector, health and higher education. Many professional services firms face a continuous and complex challenge of developing a matrix organization that serves clients globally and locally, recognizes the special need of clients and sectors and enables the growth of professional competence applicable cross-sector. We know businesses where the conflicting objectives of geographical integration and industry focus led to a sub-optimization or breakdown in the leadership, development and coordination of services. In one such business, the pre-eminence, within the matrix, given to geographical performance meant that partners with cross-geography client relationship responsibilities were under-recognized in their country or location of residence, creating a disincentive to winning and leading global programmes for clients and a consequent under-utilization of the business's potential to grow and provide globally integrated services. In another, the focus on global industries and clients outweighed the need to develop a local market that fostered the growth of local talent. There developed a breakdown of team-working between client-focused groups within the local market, with consequent impact on staff morale, development and retention, leading to a decline in business performance in the local market.

When the value attributed to one axis of a matrix outweighs that given to another, and too little attention is given to the points of intersection, there can then be a 'pulling apart' at the matrix intersection

– or systemic touchpoint – and a loss of value to the business. We have seen these tensions become more acute during times of financial crisis, such as those that the world has witnessed since 2008. In times of change or turbulence, individuals' efforts to preserve personal power and value can lead to increased competition, exaggeration of differences, conflict and internal relationship breakdown. Management of the conflict can often be overlooked or avoided because it is easier to do so; confrontation is painful and time-consuming, and focusing one's attention on client work can always be justified. In working with a number of different types of partnerships, we have been struck by the ability of the partners concerned to believe that partner-to-partner relationships were exemplary, while at the same time knowing that all was not well below the surface. Such 'wilful blindness'[14] can result in a hidden drain on collaboration and innovation which, if left un-addressed, undermines business performance and further deepens distrust between leaders and subgroups.

Paradoxically, we have found that these organizational dynamics can be just as exaggerated in those firms where the ethic of partnership and collaboration is held as being sacrosanct. Upholding the principle of partners having an 'equal' say in the business's management and future strategy can lead to an ambiguity in the exercise of power and, in many such cultures, it is not seen as legitimate to challenge another partner's behaviour. In addition, because of the pre-eminence given to client service, addressing internal conflicts can be seen to be 'time-wasting' and therefore be left to fester. This attitude, of course, does not benefit the business in the longer term, because lingering conflicts eventually drag down creativity, morale and the ability of the team at the client interface. As one client commented: 'Isn't it ironic that in a business where the ethic of partnership is so strong there can be so much competition?' The 'vicious cycle' that can emerge at the touchpoint between people in such an organizational climate is illustrated in Chapter 1, Figure 1.1, alongside the 'virtuous cycle' that is made possible through creating a collaborative climate in which differences are embraced as an opportunity to deliver ever more excellence to clients.

As we discussed in Chapter 1, one core factor determining whether a team or larger system flows into a vicious or a virtuous touchpoint cycle is the way in which the role of leadership is viewed by the senior players and the skills they apply to bring that view into reality. In the vicious cycle, leadership is seen as the attainment of personal success, or the success of one's own team – a 'heroic' form of leadership style. The attainment of personal and team goals outshines other wider objectives and can set up competition between individuals and teams, eroding collaboration and trust. In a tough economic climate we have seen such competition lead to deep division, where competition between partners encourages conflict to grow between their respective teams, and differences are exacerbated and entrenched as each group learns to attribute mal-intent to the other.

In the virtuous cycle, by contrast, leadership is seen as a shared activity and success dependent on working collaboratively to develop and achieve a shared endeavour. A trusting climate is built where individuals respect others' views and perspectives as valid and re-cognize that showing their own vulnerability can help build greater learning and shared success. This type of leadership has been called 'post-heroic' by Bill Joiner and Stephen Josephs[15] – the 'Catalyst' and 'Co-creator' leader. We examine how one business intentionally developed post-heroic leadership capacity in order to create a pro-ductive matrix-based service organization in Chapter 5.

'Outside-in' as a connecting leadership force

In our introduction to Touchpoint Leadership in Chapter 1 we note the importance of attending to the environment of any one-to-one or team relationship in order to fully understand what goes on at the touchpoint between people. Bill Critchley and David Casey talk about the value of forcing 'stuck' organizations to focus on and to understand the needs of their external world in order to help them realize the need to change the way in which they relate within.[16] More recently, Peter Hawkins[17] argues that a key first step to coaching a team lies in the team exploring the needs of its multiple stakeholders, and also taking a 'future-back' position to develop the relational dynamics within the team that will enable effective working. It often takes an external 'jolt' of this kind to loosen the existing habitual patterns so that change can be possible. An example of how one leader used an 'outside-in' perspective to galvanize the connective energy for collaboration across the competing pulls of a complex services matrix is described here.

CASE STUDY

Within a global services business, where leaders wrestled daily with the competing needs of geographically aligned P&L, the demands of globally integrated client businesses, the drive for greater innovation and growth, against the need for greater cost control and accountability, Martin had the ability to inspire hope through encouraging his leaders to face outwards. Whatever the internal struggle the business faced, he forced people to explore: 'What do our clients need and want from us?' Martin embodied the 'client voice', such that, when he entered a room, often filled with as many as 100 partners from across a region, the atmosphere shifted. But it wasn't just a mere expression of the client voice that contributed to this shift of atmosphere: Martin was respected because he knew about working with clients and led work with them; he also carried an unstinting belief in the ability of the business to meet – and even exceed – clients' demands. He said later: 'I believed that there was no business that we couldn't improve. I always believed in the ability of our people to deliver.' That belief, founded on direct experience and linked to a persistent expression of the 'client voice' in the room, gave Martin a positive posture that was easy for him to communicate – and constituted a positive and sustaining connecting energy force across complex and competing internal demands, which provided the context within which creative touchpoints of connection could be made.

Against this belief system people were encouraged to bring their best thinking within specialist service offerings and 'spark creatively' with deep sector-specific knowledge in order to develop approaches of greater value to clients.

A team-based approach to 'outside-in'

One organizational construct that aims to bring different professionals together in the service of one client system is the account team – a team of people whose role is to build business within one client system. In our work with such teams we have often found that communication focuses predominantly on operational issues and fails to draw on and capitalize the opportunity for creative learning and collaboration across the diverse sub-teams that work within one particular client.

CASE STUDY

One account team decided to invite a senior client executive to a team development event to give some candid feedback about how this team was experienced by the client, thus bringing the account team-client system touchpoint into the account team's consciousness. They were surprised when the metaphor 'comfortable old shoe' was used as part of the feedback given them. They realized that, while they had been successful in collectively creating a supportive and attentive client service, they had become complacent in their role and in so doing had lost the potential difference that they could bring to the client. The feedback galvanized them into actively exploring what more they could bring to this client system, tapping into the knowledge that was resting within each account team member and also drawing in other perspectives external to the immediate team that interacted with the client.

This team was not alone in this business in getting feedback from clients that said that they should challenge more and bring greater value through their collective difference. In their endeavour to provide excellent service to clients, and in their fear of losing business or damaging relationships, some teams were falling into the trap of being over-supportive in their relationships, arguing that a client may say that they wanted to be challenged more, but 'didn't really mean it'.

Applying the type of personal development approach described in the first section of this chapter within an account team setting, such teams were able to:

- Draw on the collective intelligence of the team to explore the issues facing the client currently and in the future.

- Use deep questioning to explore the emotional and cultural dynamic that impacted on the client's performance as well as the client's explicitly stated needs.

- Explore how each individual member could bring their experience and expertise to create optimum client value, and how they needed to team together to do this.

- Support each team member in their personal skills enhancement and so increase the capacity of each individual to bring their most creative and resourceful self to their client work.

- Develop narratives and themes with which they could challenge or reframe the client's thinking, in the knowledge that such challenges were the result of the collective thinking of the team and would therefore withstand counter-challenge.

By helping account team members in their ability to be fully open with each other – in terms of their knowledge, their insights, their emotions, their guiding assumptions and beliefs – these account teams were building greater creativity at the touchpoints within the team, through which they were able to enhance the creativity and edge in their collective touchpoint with the client system. They were also able to hone their relationship skills in a safe environment before trying them out with clients. The levels of focus in this work are represented in Figures 4.2 and 4.3.

Figure 4.2 shows the generative development cycles that are grown through this account team approach. Through discovering the client's impression of their relationship and then collectively sharing their perspectives on the client's issues and opportunities, account team members are developing new meaning for themselves and their collective endeavour. Their intra-personal development, alongside their team colleagues, helps deepen the relationships within the team and thereby enhances the capacity of the team as a whole to be different and at the same time coherent in the eyes of the client.

FIGURE 4.2   Developing the collective touchpoint of the client-facing account team

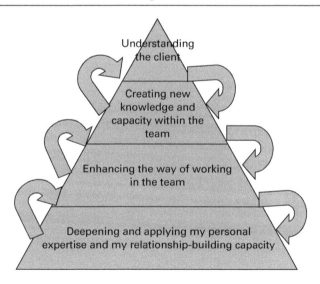

FIGURE 4.3 Account team learning at intrapersonal, team and client touchpoint

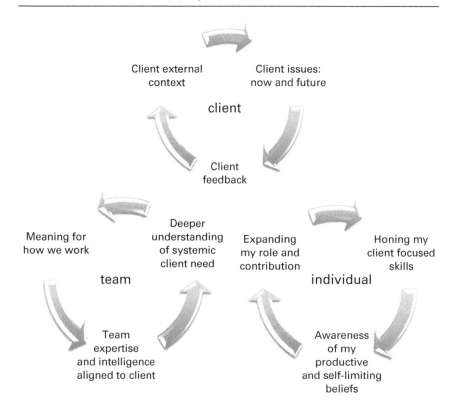

Learning about the client system through the behaviour of the team

We are frequently struck by the ability of human systems that interact with other systems, as in professional services teams and their client organizations, to mimic or mirror the dynamics of that system. Colloquially, this is often called 'going native', where the consultants and advisers cease in their ability to see the client culture from the outside, and even start to take on as their own some of the norms and behaviours of that system. They thereby lose some of their difference which in turn impacts on their potential to challenge and to create value at the touchpoint with the client.

CASE STUDY

A consulting project team was supporting a client in a major business and cultural transformation. The senior account partner had worked hard on his relationship with the senior client sponsor and was proud of his progress. He decided to run a development workshop with his team to help others buy into this relationship-building approach and thereby work to enhance the team's overall relationship with the whole client team. An inquiry involving each team member revealed some facts that were surprising to him, however: There existed deep frustration within the team at the remoteness of the senior account partner and his seeming lack of interest in the problems of the more junior project leaders. These project leaders felt torn between the demands of their middle management clients and the requirements of the consulting team's programme office.

As the team stood back and looked at this pattern of frustration with a dispassionate and objective eye, it became clear that they had started to mirror the cultural dynamic in the client system, where senior management was remote and issued edicts for improvement without attention to the problems of middle management, who in turn had to deal with demotivated and hostile employee groups, resistant to change. By adopting this mirroring stance, the consulting team had lost its ability to see the client's dysfunctional dynamic, focusing its energies instead in a parallel 'fight' with its own senior leadership. While they remained in this mirrored place they were unable to help the client system address the fissures in its own management relationships.

In psychodynamic terms, this team had been caught in a 'parallel process', where the way in which they were experiencing each other was the same or similar to the way client members experienced each other every day, as they interacted together.[18] Once the 'parallel process' had become clear to the team, they were able to explore how their greater connectedness could help the client system break out of its own fragmented leadership pattern and build greater capacity to lead the change within the business.

Using systemic polarities to spark creativity at the touchpoint

Those who lead cross-cultural teams will be aware of the ability of people with competing interests, goals, styles and priorities to polarize their differences, particularly when conditions are stressful and resources limited. This is of course true of the world in general, not just the business world, as the evidence in our perpetually fragmented political and socioeconomic world would testify. Those who have experienced the difficulties of building integrated cultures after merger or takeover, and have witnessed the emotional allegiances to legacy businesses that often persist years, even decades after the event, will also be aware of these dynamics, a point we make in Chapter 3. A depiction of this dynamic is shown in Figure 4.4.

FIGURE 4.4   Polarization of difference as a system dynamic

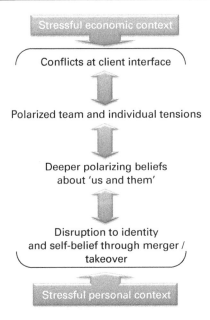

The field of gestalt therapy recognizes the creativity that can be released from identifying, exaggerating and seeking integration of polar opposites.[19] Drawing on this concept and supported by the work of cross-cultural experts Trompenaars and Hampden-Turner,[20] we have helped client-facing teams to recognize the polarizing tensions between sub-groups that are hindering performance and to work through how to reconcile these tensions. This reconciling process is founded on a spirit of respect for each position and helps build a set of actions aimed at achieving an outcome that combines the best of both. It therefore aims to unlock productive rather than destructive conflict. Our inquiry with such teams takes the following steps:

1 Build a contract that encourages a climate of openness and trust within the team.

2 Identify the conflicts existing in the client's external system and how these impact on the client's business.

3 Be open about the conflicting goals and tensions between individuals and sub-groups within the service team's own business: How much of these are 'our own' and how much constitute mirroring of the client's system?

4 Be open about the exaggerated perceptions of each sub-group and own up to the personal behaviours and sub-group patterns that contribute to these tensions. Stay with and work through the discomfort and pain that can arise from this exercise.

5 Reach agreement on how the relationship between sub-groups can be constructive at the touchpoint between them and how it can break down.

6 Explore the creative options that the team can adopt to reach reconciliation of differences at the level of:

- shared goals;
- systems of working;
- behaviours with each other;
- behaviours with clients and stakeholders.

Here again the fundamental approach rests on the development of self and other awareness within heightened systems awareness, as a catalyst in collaborative relationships. As Nevis puts it:

> *There is a premium on digging into oneself so as to be fully in touch and as clear as possible in articulating self-awareness, but an equally important effort is required for listening to and understanding others. It is this interplay of expressed awareness among the people involved that is critical for the stimulation of energy in the group.*[21]

Trompenaars and Hampden-Turner point out this recognition of difference in perspective and value needs to be followed by respect of the difference – an acceptance that there is more than one way of looking at things, and a willingness to reconcile, in order to unlock the best of each other's way of looking at things:

> (This framework) has a logic that unifies differences. It is a series of judgments that makes possible effective interaction with those who have contrasting value systems. It reveals a propensity to share an understanding of others' positions in the expectation of reciprocity and requires a new way of thinking that is circular as opposed to linear and sequential.[22]

The aspiration of firms for greater global reach, accompanied by the pressures of the market, has led the acquisitions of professional partnerships by corporations whose governance model is designed to deliver consistently to stock market expectations. The need for the acquiring enterprise to realize the benefits of its purchase often drives a focus on growth and profitability that places intense pressure on the services matrix to perform. We have worked with examples of such businesses where the need for greater transparency in financial accounting and a pressure on profitability leads to a fear among erstwhile partners that their professional and market distinctiveness will be lost. This can lead to sense of alienation within the professional community as they lose the source of their power and influence, and fear losing the source of their work fulfilment. While this can lead to a withdrawal of effort and loss of staff, those left behind often get caught in a battle between those who are driving for efficiency and those whose allegiance to the 'old ways' become ever more nostalgic.

The difficulty experienced by businesses post-merger and acquisition in valuing the contrasting perspectives, capabilities and strengths of the acquirer and acquired is a contributing factor in the failure of such transactions to deliver their anticipated value. Recognizing the importance of helping its leadership population embrace competing perspectives, priorities and objectives 18 months after takeover, one business engaged its leaders in a programme requiring them to be open about the conflicts in their roles and to recognize the business waste that can occur when critical dilemmas are avoided or allowed to fester. Using the staged 'dilemma reconciliation' process of Trompenaars and Nijhoff Asser,[23] we invited leadership groups to exaggerate their opposing positions – driving growth versus delivering profit;

meeting global targets versus meeting country targets; building people capability versus increasing efficiency – and then to develop tangible action steps to achieve an end state that drew the best of both objectives.

Most critically, the sharing of perspectives and prejudices helped people give voice to the emotional and cultural issues that underlay the tensions in the business, and enhanced the self and interpersonal awareness within leadership groups, thus helping to lay the foundation for greater leadership collaboration in future. For many partners this was the first time that they had openly and maturely addressed the conflicts inherent in the creation of a multinational consulting business through acquisition. Many expressed surprise that the programme gave them the opportunity to feel engaged and listened to and enabled them to create a meaningful set of actions and commitments to enhance leadership and teamwork going forward.

As change and organization development professionals, we know very well the mantra of the paradox of change – that change comes if you stay still. In the months after an acquisition there is rarely time to stand still and to really listen – the demands of structural and systems integration while maintaining the customer base take precedence. But our experience tells us that businesses involved in merger or acquisition would develop greater engagement and cultural integration more quickly if a higher degree of sharing and listening were built into those early days. In answer to the question: 'In retrospect, would you do anything differently?' one senior manager of an acquiring business two years post-takeover replied: 'I would inquire and listen more.'

Footnote: Partnering for client service across the business

While this chapter has focused on the touchpoint connections needed to support productive relationships with external clients, we wanted to point to the value of the principles of Touchpoint Leadership to the connection between those professionals and functional specialists who are internal to an enterprise and who provide services to internal clients. Such business partner-client relationships are often complex.

Many have dual reporting lines, both within their function and to the business unit or division they serve; and being part of the organizational hierarchy, they lack the freedom of operation – and often expression – of their external counterparts. The principle of building awareness of self and others, and of being able to stand back from the system in which they are employed, in order to optimize the value of their partnering relationship, is therefore critical. In the following example, we introduced the concept of polarity to help a business partner reframe a problematic relationship.

CASE STUDY

Paul was the head of finance operations in Europe for a global business. His personal challenge was to be more consultative in his approach to leading change, especially where he was striving to gain cooperation from people who did not directly report to him. While he was admired for his strategic vision and his drive, he had upset one or two of his colleagues by being too direct, and this had been fed back to his seniors at head office.

His relationship with Geoff, a senior finance colleague, bothered him more than any other. He worried about how Geoff would react to him, what blocks he would put in his way. He had grown to believe that Geoff was out to get him and, for Paul, that meant Geoff was harming his reputation and his career prospects. He often lost his authority when speaking to him and therefore avoided contact as much as possible. This resulted in Geoff not trusting him entirely.

Paul came to believe that Geoff was the worst thing that had happened to him since taking on his present role until, introduced to the concept of polarities and their impact on touchpoint relationships, he started to play with the idea of the opposite scenario: that Geoff was the best thing that had happened to him. Some months later he said, 'Well, Geoff was the best thing that happened to me; the resistance that he represented made us work harder to get it right. And now the change is accepted across the organization.'

By working through his antagonistic relationship with Geoff, Paul also came to realize that the tension being played out between them was actually the conflict between the head of a subsidiary business and the global finance function head – Paul and Geoff's bosses. Having recognized that the seeds of seemingly personal conflicts often arose in the wider system, Paul was able to take many types of push-back less personally. In Paul's words, 'The other day a guy was rude about my contribution and I said to myself – I am not going to let that spoil my weekend. It doesn't bother me in the same way. My confidence isn't rocked by it any more.'

Paul had used resistance and blocking as a route to engagement and at the same time he had become more connected internally – his view of himself, his life overall, his overall confidence – his authentic leadership. This helped him to manage the stressful moments in his interactions in a way that maintained his view of himself, his authority and his home life and he was able to begin to co-create an effective touchpoint.

Summary

In this chapter we have explored the nature of the relationship touch-point in outward-facing organizations and have shown the value that can be unleashed by enabling professionals to enhance their capacity for true partnership with their clients and with their colleagues. We have illustrated how the touchpoints at the client interface have the ability to bring the aspired brand alive – or to diminish it – and that these external touchpoints are also impacted by the degree of creative coherence across the complex array of internal boundaries of difference. Leaders within services businesses therefore need to act to facilitate optimum connection across these multiple points of difference if they are to build climates that foster innovation and growth to the benefit of clients and the professionals themselves. They need to be role models for creatively holding different perspectives within themselves, between themselves and others and across the firm-client interface.

So, we leave you with these questions for your own reflection:

- How far do the relationships that exist between your business and its clients, customers and stakeholders live out your intended 'brand in action'?
- How far do you personally make this brand come alive through your day-to-day connections?
- How well do your client-facing teams optimize the value of the different skills, styles and perspective of their members to provide even greater value for the clients you serve?
- How do you attend to your own learning and growth to build more depth of meaning and value in your relationships with

clients and customers at the touchpoint of your interaction with them?

● What more can you do to combine your depth of expertise with your willingness to accept 'not knowing the answer' so that you can deepen your partnership with your clients?

In Chapter 5 we move our attention to the question of developing leadership capacity within organizations, exploring the creative connections that different enterprises have developed to release and enhance leadership potential for the benefit of future business growth.

Notes

1   Hawkins develops this concept in the form of a 'relational value chain' in Hawkins, P (2012) *Creating a Coaching Culture* (New York, McGraw-Hill).

2   The tendency of professionals to see themselves in this way is referred to by David Maister (1993) in his book *Managing the Professional Services Firm* (New York, Simon & Schuster).

3   In addition, having broader non-focused conversations with clients may present problems for time accounting where conversations are not seen to be directly relevant to client work or as time-bounded business development.

4   Torbert, W and Rooke, D (2005) Seven transformations of leadership, *Harvard Business Review*, April.

5   Heron, J (1990) *Helping the Client: A creative practical guide* (London, Sage).

6   Hawkins, P and Smith, N (2006) describe this learning group intervention in *Coaching, Mentoring and Organizational Consultancy* (New York, McGraw-Hill).

7   Hawkins, P (2012) *Creating a Coaching Culture* (New York, McGraw-Hill).

8   Ibid, note 6.

9   Hanafin, J and Tolbert, M A (2006) Use of self in OD consulting: What matters is presence, in Jones, B B and Brazzel, M (eds) *The NTL Handbook of Organization Development and Change: Principles, practices and perspectives* (New York, Pfeiffer).

10   This model is built on the levels of engagement model developed by Nick Smith, in Hawkins, P and Smith, N (2006) *Coaching, Mentoring*

and Organizational Consultancy Supervision and Development (New York, McGraw-Hill).

11 The centrality of self and interpersonal awareness to emotional connection and resonance is clear from Daniel Goleman's work: *Emotional Intelligence: Why it can matter more than IQ*, (1994, London, Bloomsbury). This is developed further in his (2007) book S*ocial Intelligence: The new science of relationships* (New York, Random House).

12 Nevis, E C (1998) *Organizational Consulting: A gestalt approach* (Cleveland OH, The Gestalt Institute of Cleveland Press).

13 Cialdini sees 'reciprocation' as one of six 'universal principles' of persuasion and influence; Cialdini, R B (1984) *Influence: The psychology of persuasion* (London, Harper).

14 Heffernan, M (2011) used this term in her book *Wilful Blindness: Why we ignore the obvious at our peril* (New York, Simon and Schuster).

15 Joiner, B and Josephs, S (2007) *Leadership Agility: Five levels of mastery for anticipating and initiating change* (San Francisco, Jossey-Bass).

16 Critchley, B and Casey, D (1989) Organizations get stuck too, *Leadership and Organization Case Study*, 10 (4), pp 3–12.

17 Hawkins, P (2011) *Leadership Team Coaching* (London, Kogan Page).

18 For a description of parallel process see: Peltier, B (2001) *The Psychology of Executive Coaching, Theory and Application* (London, Brunner Routledge) and Hawkins, P and Smith, N (2006) *Coaching, Mentoring and Organizational Consultancy Supervision and Development* (New York, McGraw-Hill).

19 Clarkson, P (2004) *Gestalt Counselling in Action* (London, Sage).

20 Trompenaars, F and Hampden-Turner, C (2002) *21 Leaders for the 21st Century: How innovative leaders manage in the digital age* (New York, McGraw-Hill).

21 Ibid, note 12.

22 Ibid, note 20.

23 Trompenaars, F and Nijhoff Asser, M (2010) *The Global M&A Tango: Cross-cultural dimensions of mergers and acquisitions* (Infinite Ideas).

Building and sustaining the collaborative enterprise

05

> *Push is seductive. It creates the illusion of great power in an era when power is shifting. It can delude organizational leaders into thinking they need only roll out the new plan and massively detailed organizational blueprints will become the new scripts that everyone will surely follow.*
>
> **(HAGEL, BROWN AND DAVISON, THE POWER OF PULL[1])**

Introduction

As we look back over 25 years or so of consultancy and coaching work we are struck by the cyclic nature of organizational models and theories that have impacted our work with clients. In the 1980s we focused on processes and our ability to help re-engineer; in the 1990s we were drawn into the theories and practice of knowledge management, learning organizations and lean structures that promised to help engender and share learning and minimize waste. The financial crisis in 2008 led to a marked increase in conversations on governance and control, and the emergence of new dialogues on moral intelligence and corporate shame. Throughout it all engagement and communication have continued to be cited as a collective challenge, recognizing that an organization will be more productive if people are aligned with its strategic intent, have the space in which to learn together, connect with each other and above all create shared futures together. And as each new generation of leaders has begun to demonstrate how they might be different from the last, organizations have continued to balance the challenge of helping them to integrate with current ways of doing things while also nurturing their difference for the future development of the business.

We share a consistent vision for the organizations with which we work, viewing them as a series of interconnected relationships with the potential to become vibrant communities in which touchpoints and the relationships that help form them are central to organizational effectiveness. These are organizations in which we will find personal and collective meaning sustained by a capacity to inquire and learn and where power is synonymous with the energy we co-create, which in turn frees up the participants to act both collectively and individually.

The power of this kind of collaborative enterprise is sustained through a network of connectors, touchpoints that span the business both horizontally and vertically, requiring a quality of leadership that can attract people and resources together in such a way that they begin to work with connected passion, like living nodes in an energy network.[2] Rather than putting effort behind constantly pushing to achieve its strategic intent the collaborative enterprise relies on its capacity to pull people towards its shared goals, freeing up the blockages as they occur and paying attention to the capacity to co-create relevance and meaning through the collective work they do.

This 'pull' approach offers a challenge to our traditional forms of 'push', which according to Hagel *et al*[3] have caused us to rely heavily on a capacity to predict outcomes, and have created the need to put in place top-down controls and frameworks of roles and responsibilities to ensure full alignment to the plan. But in many cases these same frameworks have limited and constrained the power to act, leaving organizations exposed to changes in their environments that they have neither predicted nor dealt with effectively.

In this chapter we stand back from specific relationships and look at the organization as a whole, exploring how those leaders who are developing their capacity for Touchpoint Leadership are able to:

- build connective leadership both vertically and horizontally;
- catalyse sustainable habits of learning;
- trust individuals to act both responsibly and freely.

We illustrate how touchpoint leaders can help promote engagement and liberate the potential that might otherwise become trapped within the organization. We share insights into how these leaders catalyse connective and sustainable habits of learning and how they can support the continued life and growth of the collaborative enterprise by developing new perspectives on governance and control – appreciating power as the energy to act, and permission as the clarity that gives direction.

Building connective leadership – vertically and horizontally

Connecting with the 'middles' as a critical source of power and influence

Our experience has led us increasingly to include in our Touchpoint Leadership development work the group of managers and leaders who sit below the most senior levels of management. We know that these leaders are a critical source of collective power and influence and have seen first-hand how they can take ownership of significant initiatives in a way that both engages and motivates teams and groups to act. We also know that these managers can often become trapped by a pincer movement, restricted by the demands emanating from both top and bottom. Through our examples we illustrate how our clients have applied Touchpoint Leadership principles to release the energy of these 'middles' – sometimes as part of a broader top-down leadership initiative and, in one case, developing its own momentum from a clear bottom-up initiative. Engaging this group is fundamental to the success of organizational leadership.

We borrow the term 'middles' from Barry Oshry[4] who, in writing about organizational systems, warns us that this middle group can feel torn between the demands from the top and the needs of their local teams, resulting in a lack of shared common purpose and a feeling of isolation from other members of the group. This lack of connection, and a tendency to relate more closely with the teams they lead, can help compound a sense of trapped powerlessness and cause their energies to be drawn away from each other. This is often manifested in fragmentation of action across the business – often called 'organizational silos'.

We have often heard senior leaders and strategic change practitioners refer to this group as a leadership 'black hole'[5] or 'buffer' through which it is hard to drive change. This belief in part led to an enthusiasm for de-layering across industry at the end of the 20th century, seen as a means of cutting costs and enabling cleaner influencing lines from the top of the business. Taking this layer out has not always delivered the expected results however, and in some cases has served to create an enormous gap in the channels that connect strategic intent with an energy and motivation to act and deliver. We have subsequently seen a growth in enthusiasm for addressing engagement as a means of fixing the schism that these lean structures may have incidentally created, with a steady progression of programmes purporting to glue the organization together. From our perspective many of these pro-grammes have failed to ask four fundamental questions:

1 When you look across your middle leadership population, which relationships seem to have a tremendous impact on their energy and performance?

2 How much do you draw on these managers and professionals for insights into how the business is going and what is important for the future?

3 What can you learn about the quality of the touchpoints between teams and departments and what might you do to create connections for better performance?

4 How might you help create relationships that help liberate the talent and difference that sits at the middle of the organization?

We recognize that there can be significant challenges in seeking to more actively involve this 'middle' layer in the bigger picture. In those organizations where certainty and controlled leadership from the top have become the norm it can be a risky strategy to loosen hold of the reins and to ask less senior leaders what they think. In the case of one organization the incoming CEO created a high level of nervousness when he replaced his predecessor's style of command and control with a collaborative and inclusive style. His executives had become used to their habit of deferring to a more senior edict and, rather than responding enthusiastically to their new liberty, they instead found themselves joined by their common distrust and fear, and their direct reports waited for the next instructions to filter down to them. In other businesses in which we have worked, we have seen it become an accepted truth among senior leaders that more junior managers are resistant to change, unskilled or demotivated, while closer inspection reveals that these layers are only too keen to be involved – they just resent the lack of clear information given them or trust shown towards them by senior management.

One newly appointed CEO, however, decided to act differently, and to engage directly with her community of middle managers just four weeks after taking up her new role. The company had in excess of 5,000 employees and was distributed across multiple sites. Annette knew from her discussion with the chair and members of the board, prior to taking up the role, that she would need to make some critical connections happen very quickly across the organization. The disappointing results of the employee survey had repeated the dissatisfactions of the previous year and she was hearing from several sources that leadership was being cited as a critical issue.

Rebuilding organizational confidence by connecting with the energy of the middles

CASE STUDY

Rather than start her planning with her executive team, which she'd done in her previous CEO roles, Annette decided to start with a proposition of co-leadership with the 100 or more middle managers and leaders. She invited them to join her and the full executive team to participate in a half-day off-site meeting, expecting around a 60 per cent turn-out – and was delighted although slightly daunted to see over 80 per cent had in fact turned up. The energy in the room as we waited to start was tremendous – a mix of individuals taking the opportunity to connect with colleagues they wouldn't normally see and others introducing themselves for the first time.

She opened the event by instantly connecting with them, sharing a couple of stories from her own journey that gave them insight into her motivation for the leadership role and her very personal vision for their collective success. She then invited the whole group to share their own stories, casting back over a period of around five years and identifying both the highs and lows of the journey. Encouraged first to share their stories with colleagues and then depict them as pictures, we walked around the tables and the sharing started. After about 10 minutes in their small groups we invited them to transfer their pictures onto the long roll of paper we'd laid out at one end of the room, building up a collage of their collective experiences. We also invited them to do the same on the blank roll of paper at the other end of the room, this time sharing their personal and collective vision for the coming 18 months. After about 30 minutes every inch of the paper was covered and we brought the group back to their tables.

Annette then walked the length of the story timeline, slowly picking out the various images that appeared to represent significant milestones in the organization's recent history. She appeared to have an instinct for what mattered to them and the individuals who had contributed the drawings added further colour as she highlighted them and invited them to comment. The highs and lows were expressed with insight and energy, and as she walked along the years this extended leadership team enthusiastically shared the meaning behind the pictures.

As she moved to the wall depicting the future, the illustrations so clearly expressed their collective and committed energy that Annette announced her intention of sharing this sheet with the chair and board when they next met. Their connected energy had so impressed her that she was ready to express her confidence in their ability to commit to the challenges of the shared journey ahead of them.

This client had clearly taken a gamble in setting up the event in this way, and knew that it was a break with tradition to organize an off-site meeting with middle managers before the full executive away-day. But she also knew how critical it was that she helped liberate the energy of this group early on – that they needed to connect directly with her, as the new CEO, and that they needed to be able to express their own leadership voices and, above all, be able to acknowledge their shared past before engaging in creating the future together. This step was also vital in enabling the executive team to see, hear and feel the collective emotions being expressed by the middle management population.

As organizations become increasingly distributed, and as partnership and alliance become an integral part of the organizational model, we believe that this group of middle managers will need to build their capacity for Touchpoint Leadership. Their capacity to connect, vertically as well as laterally, puts them right at the core – important today because of the powerful role they play in connecting the disparate threads and increasingly significant tomorrow as they form the new leadership on which business sustainability will depend. Once liberated from any expectations of needing to be 'fixed', this population can develop a confident voice in helping co-create that future.

CASE STUDY

We facilitated the executive off-site just four weeks later, spending time prior to the meeting collating each of the executive's reflections on the 'middles' event and ensuring that each of them had an opportunity to share their own insights from the work. Although the team had already met several times in business meetings this was the first time they had spent time together focusing on themselves as a team. We spent the first part of the event encouraging each of them to share their personal hopes for the business, inviting them to share something of themselves in the process. As the energy began to build we asked them to pause and to reflect on what they'd experienced at the 'middles' event. It was critical that they connected with the emotional strength of that meeting, so that they could develop their own leadership in a way that would connect with that energy. We asked them to split themselves equally into separate halves of the room – one side representing the feelings and voices of the executive team and the other expressing the presence of the 'middles'. As they stepped into the different roles the energy increased, each side both curious and passionate in their positions. It was a powerful moment for each of them as they connected with the energy of the other, and for the rest of the time together they were able to hold on to those insights as a valuable way of measuring the likely impact of their own leadership on the business and to explore the type of leadership relationship that they needed to create together.

This example shows a CEO who wanted to create a connected leadership community right from the start. Our next story is in some ways more usual – a CEO and executive team who were experiencing some parts of their middle management team as a buffer, which slowed down their desired speed of change in the business. This has echoes of the buffer concept we explored in Chapter 3 where we saw individuals stepping into this role, but when it affects whole organizational groups then it potentially has much broader consequences.

Unblocking the barriers to sustained organizational transformation

CASE STUDY

A new CEO had recently been appointed to drive a radical transformation of the business to help secure its place in an increasingly competitive global market. The transformation required the adoption of new technology in a highly traditional business. The CEO knew that successful progress depended on the collective ability of his executive team to lead the change within the business and to overcome the rigid silos that existed between the separate divisions. In addition, as the complexity of the challenge facing the executive team became clearer, they focused their attention increasingly on the leadership capacity of the next level of managers to lead the change and bridge the silos.

To create more leadership impetus, the business had recruited a number of high-potential leaders to this management level from outside the business. But while some of these new recruits were clearly making a difference in their separate roles, it was difficult for the executives to see any significant systemic change from the recruitment campaign. The executive team recognized that they needed to find new ways to work with these leaders so that they, in turn, could galvanize the motivation and productivity of the organization as a whole.

The CEO asked us to put together a management development programme that would address the leadership capability of this cohort.

This may sound like a familiar story. We have seen other CEOs eager to drive change in the business and frustrated by the capacity of their teams to act, with their leadership teams also showing frustration at the next level. We have seen such a situation result in trust evaporating between the leadership levels and a pattern of blame growing throughout the organization, resulting in a tail-off of performance. We are also familiar with situations where a leadership development programme is seen as the answer. In the story here, it was clear that simply focusing on the individual leadership capability of this management cohort was unlikely to deliver the full extent of the transformation the business needed, and so after a series of interviews and 360-degree assessments we went back to the CEO and HR director and agreed with them that we would focus first on helping rebuild the critical connections in the organization and then address the capability issues as they became clearer. Our intention was to focus initially on:

- the connections between individuals and their self-belief;
- then the connections between individuals as members of teams and work groups; and
- probably even more critically, the connections between the leadership groups that were intended to steer the business towards its transformation.

It was only through these connections that they would liberate the individual and collective leadership capacity latent in the business. The CEO also recognized that there was work to be done with his own direct reports and asked us to include a programme of team and individual coaching for himself and his six executives.

Liberating the power to connect and step up

CASE STUDY

The CEO personally selected the 16 people who would participate in the middle manager programme, including all of the eight recently recruited high-potentials. This group of 16 were identified as needing to lead the change – and prove their worth as potential successors to the executive team. Their development needs were clearly stated as: needing to 'step up as managers and leaders', to develop better skills in communication, to challenge more, both upwards and with their own teams, and to work together in a more connected way to provide leadership across the business.

We initiated the individual coaching for this group in parallel with setting up the first group development workshop. At the first of these group sessions the fragmentation across the group was evident: many of the people in the group had not previously met. Coming together in a leadership forum in this way was unfamiliar and even uncomfortable for some, especially those with longer service. In some of the newer recruits we found a degree of disillusionment at not being able to contribute to their full potential. Some spoke of an initial period of excitement and confidence where they had felt that they could achieve change, followed by a period of withdrawal and loss of energy as they tired of being told that 'this won't work around here'. Connected to both these themes was a sense of loneliness within the group – a feeling that they were on their own, striving to achieve difficult goals, with little support from above or from peers.

Accompanying this sense of loneliness was a feeling of disconnection, compounded by overwork and frenetic activity. Everyone worked long hours, some were stressed by their lack of work-life balance, and yet there was also little sense of real progress. The productivity in the group did not seem to equate with the energy it expended.

As we invited the participants to explore collectively the impact the change programme was having on them and their teams, using a model showing emotional stages experienced in a change process, a strong common experience started to emerge. They were tangibly surprised at the consistency of concerns expressed within the group and remarked on a shared sense of responsibility for their own teams and for the collective organizational team. Each person was carrying a weight of concern and compassion for the people in their teams who in turn were being asked to take on more and in many cases to change their traditional ways of working. And yet at the same time these leaders recognized that things had to change and that the overall strategy for transformation was right for the business. They therefore felt torn, unable to reconcile these conflicting concerns.

The emerging sense of a shared experience between the leaders deepened when we asked the group to form trios and to coach each other to address leadership issues that were important to them in their role. This was challenging emotionally for several of the group because they were being invited to express vulnerability with people they did not know, who represented different interests and who, frankly, they did not yet wholly trust. But by recognizing the commonality of problems between them, and allowing themselves to help and be helped by each other, the sense of ease gradually increased. By the end of the first day the group had moved from a climate of discomfort and separation and were experiencing the power of a common emotional connection, underpinned by a mutual respect for the skills, knowledge and perspectives that were valuable in each of their roles.

It became clear to us during this first workshop that the group did in fact lack breadth in their influencing style and would benefit from developing more impact in their upwards communication. More important, it became very clear that this leadership group lacked a collective voice to speak either to their people or to the executive leadership team. Without that collective voice they could not hope to lead an integrated change programme or have the power to engage strongly from the middle of the organization.

It's not new to talk about the importance of actively engaging this middle management layer in leading the transformation programme. It has been a key feature of change management methodologies for at least three decades. But what was clearly illustrated here was the challenge faced by many organizations in accessing the richness of perspective that exists in the management levels below the top – a perspective that they gain from interacting directly with skilled operational teams, with partners and clients, and in ways that can often be more direct than those that typically exist at the top. In this type of case it is not just a question of getting such managers on board with the changes and drawing on their perspectives and experience to develop an approach that will work more effectively for the business. The bigger challenge is in helping liberate the huge potential energy that can be made available by bringing the *collective* group of managers in closer relationship with their executive leaders.

CASE STUDY

During the one-to-one coaching meetings that followed the first group development session it started to emerge that one of the reasons underpinning the lack of collaborative working between divisions was that the annual corporate plan was 'difficult to implement' properly. Individuals recounted how, towards the end of every year, the plan was drawn up in each division and then put together at executive level, with insufficient emphasis on how it could work in practice across the business and with unresolved overlaps and contradictions clearly obstructing their joined-up working. The consequence was that the divisions sometimes found themselves competing in or reworking activities, or even undertaking work that was not recognized as valid elsewhere.

As these conversations about the corporate plan developed their tone changed, moving from an expression of helplessness to a readiness to explore whether they could actually change this situation. At the next group coaching session they restarted the discussion, developing a growing belief that that this group did in fact have the power to make the change that was so critical to their ability to work together. Suddenly, people who had resisted taking on any more work because of overload were committing whole days of their time to working together to achieve a feasible and valuable plan for the following year. There was a palpable shift in the energy and motivation of several of the individuals in the group as they started to see that their influence could be so much broader. They realized that they had the power to enable greater connection, collaboration and effectiveness across the business in a way that would remove hassle, improve performance and raise the job satisfaction of their teams. The group self-selected a team to drive the development of the planning process and to talk to the executive team about their intent.

Mapping the space between the 'middles' and the 'tops'

Our experience of working with leaders in this way tells us that as the middle management cohort starts to develop their strategic leadership capacity, it is critical that they work out how to recalibrate their relationship with their executive leaders, sensitively and mindfully. Without care, this type of initiative can stimulate feelings of concern among the more senior team that they are acting above their competency level and also might be stepping beyond their authority. In the case described here we saw that there could be a risk that the renewed energy in the middle management group might spark a new sense of disconnection between the CEO and his team and their collective energy. It was therefore critical that, as part of their programme of work, they explored how they would help generate collaboration with the leadership team. Without that connection there was a risk that they could create yet another silo, highly energized but cut off from the strategic intent.

As the senior management group came together for the third workshop, we helped them look at this relationship with the executive team and the space between them.

CASE STUDY

After working with the group on their leadership styles for the first half of the morning we set up what we refer to as a 'team sculpt',[6] a way of working with a client situation that can catalyse a depth of understanding of the 'system'. Our purpose in introducing the exercise at this point was to help the group see a microcosm of the behaviours that were potentially blocking their closer connections with the executive team. We asked the group to set out chairs to represent each of the executive leaders, including the CEO. It was important that they used the placing and spacing of the chairs to represent the connections, disconnections and spaces between these 'tops'.[7]

After a brief pause we then asked each of them to very carefully place themselves alongside their executive colleagues, looking clearly at the implications of their positions and ensuring that they also depicted the relationships they might have with each other. As the group looked around they began to discern a pattern of alliances that was divisive, the withdrawal of some into the security and loyalty of their own teams and the deliberate self-projection of others to take their place alongside their executive colleagues. This was a moment when it was critical we held both the learning for the individuals and held open the space for their collective exploration. In that moment we ourselves felt a profound sense of connection with the group. The level of trust was high, as was the vulnerability of the individuals, and we knew at that point that the group had moved on. They seemed to be speaking as a collective, appeared to be developing the courage to articulate what they were noticing and learning, and as they noticed their colleagues' distress took responsibility to care for and attend to them. They were very much in control, empowered to take whatever next steps they collectively and individually agreed.

The significance of the day can be defined by reflecting on the depth of their understanding, by remembering the power of their learning, and by recalling the images of the 'system' they embodied in the room. They drew their conclusions into four insightful bullet-points:

- We are not working interdependently, and don't know how or where to do it differently.

- We don't have a mental map of our role in the transformation.

- We are being overwhelmed by the sheer volume of projects, tasks and initiatives.

- We have insufficient collective strength to enable us to regain control.

On the surface it was a simple exercise but one that clearly helped the group achieve a critical shift from one of disempowerment to an increasingly empowering perspective. It enabled the team to take its draft operational plan and successfully work through it jointly with the executive team, who then recommended their work to the board. One individual was promoted as a result of the CEO recognizing her contribution and drive to help move on the transformational agenda. Another member of the group was seconded to head up a major project on a client site. A third became a member of the executive the following year. This 'middle' group had clearly stepped into the powerful position the organization needed from them and were learning to express their collective voice in a way that would both establish their ownership of the transformation and help them engage others in its implementation.

This programme took over a year to complete, with individual development work dove-tailing with the three group workshops. In Figure 5.1 we illustrate how the learning was integrated, tracking the stages of individual insight through the right-hand loop alongside the group's capacity to grow as a collective power through the process on the left. Focusing on the left-hand circle, the group initially shared their common experience of being a senior manager within this business, starting to express and build a shared emotional connection. This connection deepened when they were encouraged to help each other address the problems and challenges that were current in their work. They learnt to value the perspectives each other brought, and the positive spirit with which it was offered, and gained confidence from finding new ways to address difficult issues together.

Through the individual coaching we witnessed a new courage to take on things that previously these individual managers had found daunting, or even pointless. They started to expand their range of influence and their ability to challenge their own leaders. As they worked intensively together to devise a way of creating a corporate plan that would be implementable, they developed an understanding of the business that went far beyond their own functional area – a breadth of perspective that was essential not only for their own roles but for their potential to advance to executive level.

Despite all the initial negative signs we saw a new group of leaders emerge – connected, energized and purposeful – and clearly operating together with:

FIGURE 5.1   Building creative connection across the 'middles'

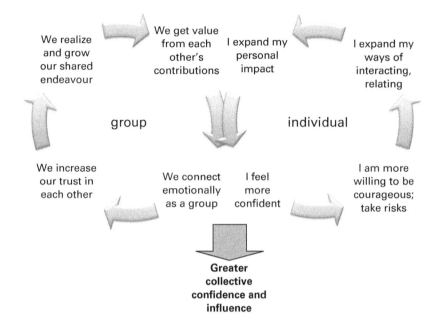

- *New emotional ground:* the group had realized that by working more collaboratively they could build greater personal and collective confidence.

- *New connective energy:* the group now showed connection and excitement in place of the scepticism and anxiety, and were now able to appreciate each other's needs and perspectives.

- *Integrated action and collaborative intent:* the group was now working as a team, understanding the issue of silo working and grasping hold of the corporate planning process to develop one that would facilitate cross-business integration in the coming year.

- *Confidence to step up:* this group of senior managers now took ownership of strategic actions, and were thus able to bring about change to benefit their teams' productivity. This gave them the perspective to challenge their own leaders – the executive team. The latter, now surprised by the energy, creativity and resilience being exhibited by the group of senior leaders, were starting to recognize how *they* needed to shift in their own strategic leadership.

This client's story illustrates how we can release both individual and collective leadership simply by enabling the power of connection. Multiple disconnects had developed in the leadership of this business through a lack of attention to the relational side of leadership – at the personal as well as the collective level – and these in turn were disabling the ability of the organization to deliver on its intent. Probably more significantly, by investing in the development of its senior managers in this way this organization was able to generate a level of collective energy for change that would sustain the organization through a series of unprecedented challenges over the next 12 months and help create a culture of inclusion, respect and trust that subsequently supported them through significant changes at the top.

Catalysing connective learning

Building a community of learning across the grain of the organization

A fundamental proposition of the concept of Touchpoint Leadership is that leaders have the power to create – or to destroy – a capacity for learning and mutual growth through the way in which they connect with others. In Chapters 2 and 3 we showed examples of leaders who challenged their own habits of relating in order to build such mutually productive relationships with their colleagues and put forward the concept of reciprocal exchange as an essential quality of Touchpoint Leadership.

In this chapter we illustrate how this capacity for connective learning is pivotal in creating the collaborative enterprise, ensuring that the learning and insights of individuals, teams and groups touch at the very point at which they can add value to the business. We focus on developing habits of learning that constantly check and challenge the current organizational knowledge and which engender the confidence and courage to express out loud the new insights that emerge. These in turn become rich sources of action for the business. So in this section we demonstrate how leaders have enabled a habit of learning that begins to connect whole groups across the organization, drawing them together as they exercise the qualities of inquiry and dialogue as an essential 'pull' behaviour of Touchpoint Leadership.

Below we track the story of one client, a professional services business, that created a new matrix structure to build resource strength and flexibility across the organization. Prior to the changes, consulting services had been organized in a way that aligned them to the client sectors they served, and the consulting staff reported to and were rewarded by those sector divisions. However, the business realized that holding consultants in small sector-focused 'client groups' presented challenges for project resourcing, capability development and the career flexibility of its consulting workforce. These issues were magnified when market challenges placed constraints on resource numbers. A new, horizontal service line structure was therefore introduced, cutting across the vertical sector-focused structure. The ambition was to build a service line community of practice that fostered skill development and learning in a way that was attractive and engaging to staff wherever their client work resided.

CASE STUDY

As the year developed, the leadership of the business came to realize the impact on morale of these structural changes. The introduction of new processes for determining who would appraise performance and determine reward threatened people's sense of 'home' within the business and, for some, their group identity. Leadership started to invest time in an engagement and communication programme aimed at helping people understand the rationale and value of the changes, an initiative that did not significantly improve staff feedback.

When we met Richard, the head of this new consulting service line, he had already given a lot of thought to his leadership approach and to how he needed to shift his own ways of communicating to the 300 people in his service line in order to help them feel a restored sense of belonging and optimism. He told us that he had started this personal transition by reflecting first on what he remembered moved him when he was a junior consultant in the business:

> The communications that I remembered were those that showed that the leader had some affinity with me as a junior member of the firm – maybe it

*was a handwritten note, or because they remembered my name out of the
hundreds that worked there.*

*Then I thought about how I want to be communicated to now: the big stuff
doesn't work for me; I cannot stand pre-canned voicemails as a motivator and
formal e-mails are just impersonal – for information only. It is not just about
my communicating with them top-down; it is also about their connecting with
me, bottom-up. I need to find out: is my message received? Am I misquoted?
Misunderstood? I don't want a group of 'yes' people. You need to look at the
sheer complexity of the team. They have such different expectations. What
matters to them? Many don't want a vision – they want their IT kit to work....*

*I wondered, 'How do you create a climate where they spark off each
other?' I started to have smaller conversations of 15–20 people and people
started to put their hands up. I always respond to e-mails and I started to
bring people who contacted me into my network. It was ad hoc. Gradually
I am building a network of like-minded individuals, starting to weave in their
ideas and act on their recommendations, draw on their advice. They of course
talk to their peers. If I can get more touchpoints... I can build an ecosystem. I
don't care about the grade or gender or anything – I care about what they are
bothered and excited about. Also I make sure I see them on their turf. I see
the work they want to talk about. Stories are a good way of communicating.*

This style of communication was not confined to face-to-face meetings: Richard
sent informal communications from his Blackberry, always speaking about
important matters and conveying authority, mingling that authority with informality
and intimacy. He went on to say:

*People remember stories; history was passed down in stories and parables.
I wanted my Blackberry messages to be interesting, relevant, timely and
personal – I try to tell it like a story, in an engaging way.*

*I always think about the type of person who is receiving my Blackberry
e-mails, as well as the quality of the connection I make. I try to give them
something they weren't expecting. I look to invest something else into the
relationship so that I can deliberately make a connection with people –
and they often respond really positively. After one e-mail about leadership,
50 people replied sharing something about their own experiences.*

It was clear from the positive feedback this senior leader was receiving that this
type of approach was resonating within the business. People appreciated the
informality of his communications and the fact that he met them on their own turf,
spoke their language and demonstrated that he too was involved in client work.
He was a senior person with whom they could identify and relate. But while his
personal presence was helping to open up new channels of understanding, these
touchpoints, or moments of exchange, were vulnerable to a number of sources of

interference. First, he could not reach all 300 people face-to-face very quickly, especially given his own client-facing responsibilities. Second, within a matrix organization it is difficult for a single leader to have a monopoly of influence – consultants still interacted every day in sector and client-facing teams. Third, the newness of the organization structure meant that old power relationships had not been changed, and fourth, the wider organization rhythm was strongly influenced by an emphasis on improving performance and cost control. This had the potential to work against investment in people development, which was critical to developing a consulting capability of which the business could be proud.

While he had growing confidence that the leadership approach that he had adopted was having a positive effect, Richard knew that he would not be able to create the vibrant consulting community that he aspired to unless he helped free up the leadership capacity of senior practitioners in the business. He therefore established a reinforced leadership team, drawing the heads of the individual practices together with the client group consulting heads, and increased the amount of time available to them to exercise this leadership role. He invited us to work with him and his team to see how the principles of Touchpoint Leadership could help them embed the community of consulting practice within the business.

Enabling a new leadership team to move from formation to high performance is always challenging. But building a team to lead a newly created axis within a matrix organization, which runs against the grain of historical sources of power, influence and allegiance, is far tougher. The challenge was to form a team that would spearhead a community of practice where the centre of gravity for most of its members came from their client work and sector-based specialization. Understandably there remained ambiguity about how the new organization would work in practice, how performance would be assessed and rewarded and careers managed.

Richard was aware that his aspirations for the consulting business, and his clarity of vision for what needed to be done, could get in the way of his new leaders stepping up to the task. But at the same time he was impatient – unless the team provided clarity fast, and delivered tangible results, he feared that the new organization could unravel or not be given a chance to be successful. Staff attitude surveys were showing that others were also impatient for clarity about the value of the new structure for them. It was essential for Richard to get the right balance between a leadership style that provided clear and practical direction, and one that enabled the team to step into their leadership roles to visualize and design the way forward themselves. But he still wasn't sure what the winning combination of tight versus loose might be, and anticipated that switching his style might cause some confusion.

As we started to work with the team, we noticed there were many tasks being initiated, many great ideas for action, but also an incipient tiredness and frustration at lack of progress. There was a feeling that the work of the new team was 'pulling people away' from the *real* work of the business – that of serving clients. The result was that alongside real passion and creativity we witnessed a passivity and optionality. It was also evident that Richard's need to have faster impact than was currently possible was showing up in his demeanour with his team:

> *I realized that my actions were not aligned with my words. I wanted them to be engaged but my body language was showing something different. I was bringing my frustrations into the room. It is hard to step out of this pattern when you are in the middle of it – but it is vital to get an objective view that makes you think about how others see you.*

It was clear that real progress would not be made unless Richard was able to work with his team to develop shared ownership of the leadership task. This would best be initiated by getting candid views from each of them of the challenges they faced and how they could best address them. A process of development was initiated that evolved into four main phases of growth for the team.

CASE STUDY

1. Co-creating clarity of purpose

An interview programme involving each team member unearthed the challenges they were experiencing in establishing new channels of influence within an existing and well-oiled organizational system. While pleased about their new leadership position, and committed to building a consulting capability, several still felt they lacked the authority to influence people to take action outside of their client work. Some felt conflicted in their own roles and objectives, doubting whether it would be possible to create a consulting service line structure within a system that was strongly aligned to driving performance within client sectors. These doubts spread to concerns about whether the leadership team could operate as a team if its needs were different and opportunities for interdependency limited.

The act of taking time out to acknowledge that this group of leaders, like their junior colleagues, lacked clarity was a vital first step in building confidence in the group. It also provided Richard with the feedback he needed to be directive about its first task – to create the operating model by which it would manage and review its performance. But while he was directive about *what* was done and the basic performance indicators that would be used, he handed the task to the team so that they could co-create the model, and therefore design *how* they would lead the business of the service line.

2. Reframing the role of leadership

At the same time we encouraged the team to consider the possibility that the personal qualities of leadership that might be needed of them in this new environment might be different from those they had used in the past. These leaders would need to lead through influence across the formal authority structures, and create collaborative connections to build a coherent rather than a divisive community of practice. As two members of the team told us: 'I am beginning to see leadership here as much more about sparking connections with people rather than controlling them – the challenge is how I let go to allow people to contribute fully.' 'We need to decide what kind of leadership we need to create – how to influence without strong control.'

We asked the team to start to explore the critical points of connection that they needed to influence and to support and challenge each other in how to make these touchpoints more productive. In addition we helped each leader start his or her own leadership development journey. We kicked off a one-to-one coaching programme to help them enhance their self and interpersonal awareness, and encouraged them to draw on the reflective exercises shown in Table 5.1 and to journal their progress.

3. Giving the space to learn and lead

As the role of the team became clearer and they began to take forward their plan of action, it was evident that the leaders were gaining confidence. But it was also apparent that Richard's clarity about what needed to be achieved was leading to impatience at the pace of progress and this in turn appeared to be getting in the way of his reports contributing to their full potential. It seemed to be a good time to stand back to see how well they would step into their leadership roles. Client commitments and the need to take time away from the office gave him the opportunity to step back and see whether a lighter leadership approach would facilitate greater creativity within the team.

Within a culture where 'it was important to get things right before taking action' this stepping back was a bold step. And yet Richard was delighted to see that it had just the impact he hoped for – a core group of the team started to lead communications and capability development initiatives in his absence, such that

TABLE 5.1 A reflective framework

Touchpoint Leadership Principle	Questions for reflection
Lead by bringing personal values and purpose to your leadership role in a way that engages and inspires others	• What are you passionate about in your role? • What values guide you as a leader? • How far do you use these to inspire or encourage others?
Be aware of the impact of your own style, behaviours and habitual patterns on others and their impact on you	• What aspects of your leadership and teamworking style engage and motivate others? • What aspects may sometimes prevent others giving their best?
Consciously learn and grow in your connection with others	• How do you want to grow as a leader while being part of this team? • What have you learnt so far about yourself from your work in this role/team?
Make the most of people's different approaches and contributions at the moment you connect with them – to release energy, creativity and engagement	• Are you aware of the impact you have on others at the moment you connect with them? • When you pay attention to that, what do you notice? • What do you change, or do?
Identify the most important value-creating touchpoint connections in the business	• Who are the most important people to whom you need to relate in order to fulfil your leadership role? • What is the nature of your relationship with them? What needs to shift and how?
Encourage others to embrace and learn from difference	• How well do you encourage others to collaborate across the team and the business and to learn from the difference it brings, and to build a learning community?
Create a trusting climate where people are empowered to act freely, accountably and interdependently	• What do you do to create a climate of trust, where people take initiative through their own free will, in the interests of the business? What more can you do?

Richard was able to see that his own leadership was having greater rather than less impact on the business than before.

4. Creating a leadership learning hub

While individual leaders were engaging well in their part of the organization and the tasks of the team were being progressed, questions started to resurface about the strength of purpose of the service line and the role of the leadership team. It seemed its authority was still not seen as strong enough when compared with that of the client groups. Through conversations with team members it became evident that while it was seen to be competing with the client groups for power or voice it could not be successful. A far more important question emerged: 'How can we build a culture of learning between us, as leaders of this practice, and with our people, which enables the consulting service line to grow, develop and serve the business more effectively?'

Therefore the ability of these leaders to build relationships with each other that facilitated learning and growth was key to role modelling and catalysing a culture of learning with the service line overall. They started to invest time in getting to know each other more deeply, in understanding the passions and values that they brought to their work so that they could start to bring to life a new way of being within the business. And this led to a redesign of the way in which they spent time with each other, minimizing the collective time spent on reporting and progress chasing that was the normal way of doing business, and maximizing the time spent on creating new programmes and approaches that would significantly benefit the wider community. As one team member put it:

> *I strongly believe in making the organization a better, happier place to work. Organizations treat people like machines – I believe that they should be treated as human beings. But in my need for high standards I know I can drive for perfection and I am not then allowing them to grow and learn – I am not showing the full power of my values to them. If we can together help this business be a better place for people to grow, that is very exciting.*

At this stage in the work the leadership team committed to a two-year development programme, recognizing that embedding the new learning culture, which itself ran across the embedded culture of the organization, would take time and persistence. The leadership being shown by this group had already been lauded throughout the senior ranks of the business, and the signs were that people were beginning to feel increasingly part of a practice that cared about their development. The vision and determination of one leader to step out of the habitual way of doing things, to trust in the potential of a new team and to gradually encourage them to similarly step out, had clearly helped co-create new patterns of influence, collaboration and growth.

Learning to create succession

This trust in the potential of people to step into the unknown – to risk to be different – in order to catalyse change was illustrated again to us when we worked with the European leadership team of a global business. They were in the process of creating a high-potential pool as part of their succession planning process. They had re-organized the business two years previously, moving from a country-based structure to an organization divided into three regions. They now faced two interrelated challenges: they did not have a succession planning process that would ensure a next generation of leaders capable of taking the lead in Europe, and they did not know who these potential leaders might be. They set out to identify 30 people whose performance and leadership assessment results suggested high senior leadership potential.

CASE STUDY

The European leadership team took two key decisions. First, they set up a series of cross-Europe leadership meetings designed to involve the selected high-potential group in the strategic development of the business. They invited the group to participate in a range of conversations through these meetings, intending to expand their field of vision and expose them to new connections. These were very new experiences for the group and they were extremely energized by the opportunity to connect and share their questions and insights with the leadership team. The catalytic effect went beyond the conversations, though. Their impact stretched to the leadership team itself, and they found that they too were developing new insights that would ultimately enrich the quality of their collective decision making. They had begun to build a community of learning, the exchange between the two groups inadvertently providing the foundation for an ongoing dialogue.

Second, and in parallel with the expanded leadership meetings, the business invested in a highly intensive development programme for the 30 to help them develop the leadership skill and resilience necessary for the next step up. This programme, built on a foundation of self and interpersonal awareness, enabled the participants to connect their expanded field of vision with increased skill in engaging and inspiring others.

When the head of the European business attended the final review of this programme six months after its inception he no longer assumed the driving seat; instead he sat and listened for 45 minutes to the thoughts and insights of the senior leaders. Only then did he start to engage in a dialogue about the future of the business.

Although initially intending to invest solely in a succession planning process this business actually achieved a systemic shift in its leadership through the quality of dialogue it was able to engender. By listening attentively it expanded the field of trust between the top team and a highly valued cadre of leaders drawn from across the business. It also shifted the nature of the relationship between the CEO and this high-potential group, rebalancing a previous tendency for the CEO to speak while others listened with a new pattern of input and listening held in comfortable exchange. We also have clear evidence that this new habit of learning directly contributed to the continuing success of the business. A few months later this expanded leadership community successfully rose to the challenge when called on to support a major transformational change, and the CEO was able to depend on them to help build engagement and connection across the key divisions within the region.

This capacity to learn and adapt and to constantly challenge the knowledge that is applied to the organization's decision-making activities is critical to ongoing value-creation in the business. As relationships become the connective links across boundaries new perspectives and value systems will impact the meaning that emerges at the touchpoint. Leaders will need to ensure that these many and diverse perspectives join up coherently and meaningfully, providing a new framework for action that makes sense both locally and collectively. It is also critical that leaders enable their teams to cascade a climate of learning that encourages creative connections beyond the boundaries of their own teams, reaching out to engage in learning conversations with clients, customers and business partners who sit at the edge of their business.

In their exploration of the globally integrated enterprise, Lojeski and Reilly[8] propose that we should enable the creation of 'virtual ensembles' in place of defined team structures, emphasizing the need to enable these fluid entities to connect via technology and in the spirit of achieving a shared outcome. These group members are no longer tied to each other through traditional organizational means and therefore the need to acknowledge new forms of motivation, evaluation and reward is increasingly critical to their success. Like them, we recognize that in many cases the work practices and mental models about what encourages people to cooperate have not kept up with these new, fluid structures and we therefore encourage our clients to consider the following as essential when setting out to enable similar touchpoint learning communities:

- an investment of time and energy to build the kinds of connective relationships that both integrate individual contributions and maximize the collective outputs;
- a preparedness to allow hubs of learning activity to co-create new insights and potentially challenge the dominant knowledge holders;
- a shared capacity to work with diversity and difference in a way that maximizes all contributions to enhance rather than hinder business performance.

They will also need to deal with an increasing level of ambiguity, as well as develop the capacity to accept that they will not always know. We recognize that it is probably counter-intuitive to encourage 'not knowing', but the last few years of global development have indicated that in fact we often do not know and must instead develop our capacity to deal with the emergent. The real challenge lies in remaining connected and engaging in thinking together. Working wisely is key – fostering learning habits and asking: how can we accelerate our learning while at the same time slowing the pace to make space and time for reflection and connection, thereby maximizing the strategic impact of one person's learning for the benefit of the collective whole? This is conscious Touchpoint Leadership – self-aware and self-correcting.

For some organizations it can be an enormous challenge to re-orientate their culture like this. One client shared his reflections on the way his executive colleagues struggled to come to terms with the philosophy of their newly appointed CEO. The new CEO believed firmly in a culture of collaboration and shared learning and invited his executive team to co-create alongside him rather than continue to give them the firm direction his predecessor had done. He had to learn quickly how to deal with the negative responses it engendered as they struggled to make sense for themselves, not knowing how to take the freedom being offered and for some time remained trapped in their habitual disempowerment.

From data collection to collective knowing

CASE STUDY

This was an organization that had enjoyed significant success over many years. It had developed an extremely strong focus on execution that seemed to ignore the value of relationships. The company operated at such a fast pace, creating connections only on the surface level, that it felt justified in putting execution very firmly first.

Relationships had never been viewed as key and there had never been a huge reliance on them. Although customer feedback had continued to highlight issues engendered by its culture the warnings had not been considered serious enough to warrant change. However, a changing economic climate and the emergence of new competitive markets had caused business performance to deteriorate and management had discovered fundamental flaws in their philosophy: there were insufficient big relationships, external and internal, to carry them forward as a big player with bigger growth challenges. The level of innovation they needed had increased, the risks in their decision making were growing and the impact those decisions might have were multiplying – all of this highlighting the need for bigger, deeper relationships.

The developing organizational view was that the previous CEO had an incredible business brain and had held the company's knowledge bank. He related to his executives via hub and spoke, and ensured he recruited fantastic executors of strategy. And he pulled them into line if they erred. Knowledge sat firmly within the domain of this CEO, and relied on a constant flow of data from the functional and geographic offices, both global and local, to feed its hunger. The firm leadership of the business depended on a highly efficient, one-way process of taking in data, digesting and analysing it, and then applying it to top-down decision making.

The continuing success of the strategy depended on the activities of staff across the business being aligned to and fully compliant with the needs for supply and demand. Up to that point the strategy had seemed to serve its purpose, a highly efficient transactional model that kept the organizational engine running. However, in the face of significant change and challenge, this transactional model was no longer sufficient.

The new CEO required a very different team around him; he needed people who would support him, collaborate, work together and be as one. It was a slow start – there were lots of senior people looking for direction because they'd been developed in that mould. But little by little the new CEO began to ignite small fires of energy that began to pull people towards his new vision and culture. Those who responded to his invitation found they had aligned views, the same agenda, were prepared to take the conversation forward, and above all had already begun to develop longer-lasting relationships. There was a view, however, that some executives had depended on the previous CEO to such an extent that they had lost the ability to think and make sense freely, depending instead on his interpretation and sense-making before leading the implementation. The organization needed to grow in emerging markets but could not innovate quickly enough. Senior leaders were waiting for direction at the very moment when their teams were waiting for direction from them. As the new CEO started to create a new more collaborative approach to decision making there was a risk that, rather than this being perceived as the right answer to the business's challenge, he would be seen as lacking the strength to lead them to new growth.

The client knew that they had to start by moving from the dominant patterns of command and control to the collaborative and co-creative behaviours that in turn would accelerate the re-engagement of the global leadership communities. These groups were geographically spread and had a high dependence on virtual networking. We had already discussed the potential impact of helping identify the critical touchpoints across the global space and shared the concept of 'creation spaces'[9] with them as a way of creating the level of attraction that would draw the learning energy together. These creation spaces are defined by Hagel *et al* as attracting performance-driven teams to foster rich interactions both within and across other teams, and highlight the need to pay attention to three critical components: the participants, the interactions they might develop and the environment that would be necessary to make them work.

Our encouragement was to invite the executive team to treat participating individuals as co-creators, respecting the diversity and distinctive needs of each of them and helping engender an environment in which they would be both encouraged and enabled to access and attract the support and resources they needed locally. We shared the principle of exchange as a means of helping rebuild critical connections and create a means of bringing people together to learn – and unlearn – and in a way that would enable them to co-create their leadership position. This was very different from the type of trans-actional model this company was used to but they agreed that it would be the most effective way of helping generate new connections and provide the platform for co-creation.

Since working with this client we have observed an increasing number of organizations seeking to move from 'push' to 'pull' strate-gies, and even more are questioning their ability to fully realize the collective knowing of their organizations. Learning to listen is simply a first step – and a critical step – as they begin to open up the possi-bilities through new habits of dialogue and inquiry, supported by a commitment to extend these creative connections across teams and out towards clients, customers and business partners where mutual learning is becoming a core principle of sustainable engagement.

Trusting to act responsibly and freely

Many of the stories in this book have illustrated what we observe as a continual struggle in organizations between individuality and conformity, between the recognized need to recruit and develop originality and difference and the realized need to homogenize diver-sity in a way that it can be managed and directed to deliver results. Often we hear the options expressed as polar opposites, balancing the choice between 'a freedom to invest in high-risk innovation' and a strict adherence to 'governance and cost control'. One client described their specific challenge as needing to explore how they might balance the need for compliance (they work in a highly regulated section of the energy sector) and the agility and pace that might enable them to define the future (relating to the unpredictable challenges of climate change).

As we introduced the Touchpoint Leadership concept in Chapter 1 we illustrated the pivotal role of trust in enabling connected learning and growth. In our conversations with executives we are often told that 'you earn trust', that 'you can't give someone trust until they prove that they can handle it'. We understand this sentiment, but we also believe the converse to be true – that the more you trust responsible people, the more they will offer in return. Without this willingness to trust we see situations like those described earlier in this chapter, where a CEO's lack of trust engendered a culture of compliance and a dampening of individual initiative that was slow to respond to a new collaborative leadership style. We also have the example of the loss of capacity when the 'middles' in an organization were stifled by their CEO's lack of trust in them, and even began to doubt their own abilities to perform. Experiences such as these tell us that if we focus too strongly on managing the risk of what might go wrong, building in checks and balances into our processes and relationships, then we actually encourage more distrust and so continue to feed the negative cycle. And of course we have illustrated where the converse is true – where a leader's trust in his people helped create a spirit of optimism and energy as they learnt to balance autonomy with interdependence, equality with control and authority.

Throughout the book we have offered the concept of Touchpoint Leadership as a way of stepping out of such polarized tensions as 'control versus freedom' by encouraging leaders to focus on relationships in a way that will catalyse, accelerate and sustain business change, maximizing and encouraging the unique qualities that people can bring. In this chapter we have looked at a business that enabled its middle manager group to connect and to find its collective leadership capacity; we have seen how a leadership team grew a culture of learning across the grain of the organization as a means of connecting capability development and growth. In each of these cases, freedom to act was key. These organizations have been able to step out of the either/or debate and have developed environments in which freedom *and* responsibility combine to liberate their people to act.

Of course, a leadership team needs to have the confidence that any one area of the business will not go off at a completely different tangent that will be harmful or toxic. The quality of the relational holding space is key in setting the parameters for individual leaders to fully realize the tension and spark of the touchpoint as a rich source of insight, action and also accountability.

Our work has also shown the importance of helping leaders develop the clarity and perspective to discern the personal and collective patterns in the system so that they are able to steer their own way through the complexity and ambiguity, and through their leadership transform the connections between individuals, teams and the sub-units that make up the system. As they generate personal, collective and organizational coherence at the touchpoint they in turn help co-create a sense of meaning that frees up others to act responsibly, both together and separately. If they get it right, this freedom to 'be' will provide opportunity to foster innovation, engender the capacity to improvise and facilitate independent thought within a shared responsibility to the organization's overall business endeavour.

Conclusion

In this chapter we have illustrated how different organizations have applied the concept of Touchpoint Leadership to liberate their collective leadership capacity to bring about productive change. We recognize that continuing pressures to grow, perform and deliver may well result in leaders reverting to tactics of control in the hope that they will be able to turn up the dial on performance. At the same time it is highly likely that they will frustrate the efforts of those seeking to deliver, unwittingly drive greater internal fragmentation and ultimately erode the trust and hope that is in fact critical to their success.

We therefore encourage leaders to explore how they can address their business challenges by looking through a new lens at the potential of their people to lead, and share these final questions:

- How might a new generation of leaders develop their collective capacity for relational leadership?

- What might they understand and experience as the touchpoint, and how might Touchpoint Leadership help liberate their ability and willingness to contribute in a new way?

- How can you encourage new generations to want to bring their uniqueness to the benefits of our enterprises?

- What if we were to help the new generations of leaders develop a holistic understanding of themselves, the space they inhabit, the impact they have on others?

- What if we were able to develop a greater systemic perspective, and help future generations live and work in a wholly connected and joined up way?

- What impact might a shift in perspective such as this have on broader communities and society in general?

In the final chapter we invite you, as a leader who faces these challenges, to take time to look at your own leadership and start to explore how touchpoint principles can help you start to address these questions with renewed energy, insight and optimism.

Notes

1   John Hagel, John Seely Brown and Lang Davison offer the concept of 'pull' as a powerful way of understanding and working with the need to attract people in such a way that we increase our collective understanding and effectiveness and turn uncertainty into opportunity – the smallest of moves able to achieve outsized impact. *The Power of Pull: How small moves, smartly made, can set big things in motion* (2010, New York, Basic Books).

2   Hagel *et al*, ibid.

3   Hagel *et al*, ibid.

4   Writing about 'system blindness' in organizations, Barry Oshry groups patterns of behaviour into four definitions: tops, middles, bottoms and customers and then encourages us to work with these insights to challenge the stuck and habitual behaviours that will potentially block the effectiveness and ultimate success of the organization. *Seeing Systems: Unlocking the mysteries of organizational life* (2007, San Francisco, Berrett-Koehler).

5   In his work on leading change, Daryl Conner describes 'black holes' as forming where middle managers do not adequately support change, possibly as a result of unintentional confusion, covert sabotage or simply the enormity of the pressures they are under. Like the black holes in space these potential chasms in the business have the capacity to distort or even swallow up the change effort. *Managing at the Speed of Change: How resilient managers succeed and prosper where others fail* (2006, New York, Random House).

6   Described by Peter Hawkins and Nick Smith as a means of re-enacting a team client situation in *Coaching, Mentoring and Organizational*

Consultancy: Supervision and development (2006, London, Open University Press).

7 'Tops' are part of the Oshry model referred to in note 4.

8 Lojeski, K S and Reilly, R R (2008) *Uniting the Virtual Workforce: Transforming leadership and innovation in the globally integrated enterprise* (New York, Wiley).

9 'Creation spaces' are described by Hagel *et al* as having the potential to deliver a very different form of performance improvement curve – one that will rise in proportion to the number of people collaborating. Rather than a redefinition of the 'learning organization' these emerge as ecosystems across businesses and catalyse learning as a by-product of their collaboration to achieve performance improvement (see *The Power of Pull* in note 1).

06

Developing touchpoint mastery

> *I have realized that I cannot change others – I have to start with myself. If I defend less, and carry my own expertise with less push, I am open to the needs and perspectives of others and the difference they bring. Then together we can work to see how we can contribute to the bigger picture in this business, one conversation at a time.*
>
> **(INTERNAL BUSINESS PARTNER)**

Introduction

Throughout the five preceding chapters of this book we have invited you to accompany us on a reflective journey. We started by introducing the concept of Touchpoint Leadership and the three developmental domains – connecting with a deeper self, connecting in relationship and connecting others – that we believe are at the core of a collaborative leadership practice that both values and leverages the best of difference.

In Chapter 2 we gave illustrations of how leaders with whom we have worked have grown their capacity to unlock the potential in others through exploring the values, passions and influences that together define their own ability to connect in productive dialogue.

Chapter 3 brought to life the potential of 'pivotal relationships' within organizations as a powerful means of contributing to, or hindering, the relational energy needed to drive performance. These illustrations shone light on how leaders need to be aware of the potential for waste at the touchpoint and highlighted some of the risks inherent in relationships that do not attend to connection and mutual growth. In Chapter 4 we looked at the touchpoint that happens at the point of connection between client-facing staff and their clients, and the impact of touchpoint experiences on the reputation and brand image of a services firm. The same experiences can be tracked at the point of connection between customers and suppliers and within internal partnering relationships. We went on, in Chapter 5, to examine how leadership teams have sought to build collaborative cultures through creating the conditions for connection and learning across organizational layers and silos, and we have pointed to ways in which the concept and practice of Touchpoint Leadership can further catalyse the building of trust and engagement in business, and with even greater hope in our global and social communities. Throughout the book we have endeavoured, through reflective questioning, to encourage you to bring your own experience to your reading so that the illustrations and models presented might spark new thinking and insight in a way that provides value to your own leadership.

In this final chapter we return to the three developmental domains of Touchpoint Leadership and provide a framework, built on a cycle of reflection and action that can serve as a set of guiding principles to developing and enhancing your own leadership practice. Starting with a reminder of the three domains and their scope, we refer you again to the model we introduced in Chapter 1, included in Figure 6.1.

FIGURE 6.1   The concept of Touchpoint Leadership

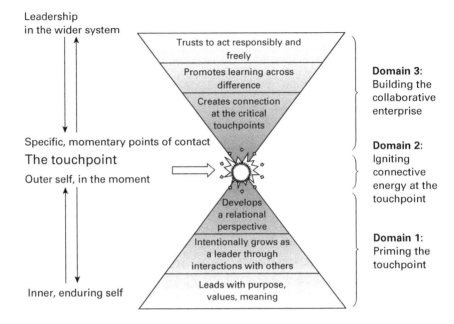

In summary, the three domains require leaders to:

- Enrich their understanding and insight into their inner self – the enduring and evolving pattern of their life's experiences, values, beliefs, assumptions and deep purpose – and be more conscious and mindful of how that inner self influences and is manifested in their leadership role, in the way in which they make sense of the world, and how it impacts each moment of contact with others. We refer to this as *'priming the touchpoint to become relational'*.

- Be constantly aware of the personal presence necessary to generate creativity and mutual exchange at the touchpoint, helping release productive energy at each point of connection, and being continuously ready to learn, adapt and flex from each relationship in the system. This is what we refer to as *'igniting connective energy at the touchpoint'*.

- Identify the incremental business value that can be created from acknowledgement and connection of all aspects of difference across the organization, engendering a culture of learning and trust and *'building and sustaining the collaborative enterprise'* as a whole.

A framework for learning

Before we look in detail at the types of questions and exercises that can be used to help focus on each of these three developmental domains, we first want to share some guiding principles that we have found can accelerate personal insights and help integrate the new learning into new behaviours.

Creating new ways of being and relating is not easy: it requires us to stop doing things that are familiar to us, to interrupt habits that have served us well and have contributed to our success to date, and to be prepared to try an alternative way. These principles are therefore built on a three-stage cycle[1] of pausing and attending, reflecting, and acting on new insights in a way that helps realize the new possibilities. Underpinning each cycle is an ability to bring attention to what matters most.

1. Pausing and attending

Although it may feel countercultural we always recommend that leaders find a way of freeing up at least 30 minutes a day to simply pause. Silent pauses built into the daily routine offer a way of freeing the mind from its incessant activity and enable leaders to bring their attention back to what matters most: for them personally, for the people they connect with, for the organizations they lead.

This discipline of creating time and space to pause and think is fundamental to new learning. First, it gives time to stand back and to see the patterns and activities in your life from a new perspective. Second, it enables you to access the restorative energy that is critical to effective functioning of the brain and the body[2] and fundamental to supporting efforts for change. And third, by being prepared to pause and let go of the immediacy of the present, you begin to choose where to shine the light. To really leverage the full value of the moment we recommend first attending to what is happening from the inside out – noticing your feelings, your bodily responses, your thoughts and worries, passions and excitements – and then from the outside in – the expressions, actions and reactions of others, the patterns of behaviour in groups and systems, the pressures from outside the system. This quality of attending requires an openness of mind to new possibilities, a refined tuning in to the subtleties that often get missed in the normal course of a day's hectic business, and above all a readiness to accept the insights that can flow from the time-out.

We refer to it as a 'practice of attending' and recommend it as a daily discipline that can be the first powerful step in creating both personal and collective change.[3]

2. Reflecting

Once leaders have created the space for slowing down and stepping back we encourage them to take the time to reflect, to take notice of what emerges, remaining curious about the thoughts and emotions that flow in and then back out again. In this way they hear the new questions that arise, the recollections and patterns that might now have new meaning in today's context – while at the same time holding it lightly in a way that allows them to extract what is most relevant and important. It is all rich data, some of it more valuable in the here and now, and some of it likely to become significant in the process of development. It can start to inform a leader's sense of how they want to be and how that might be translated into reality, to provide a mental template against which to see new experiences.[4] Journalling observations and thoughts can offer a way of returning to the data at a later date, drawing new conclusions from the experiences as you view them through a lens formed from more recent insights.

3. Acting on new insights

Throughout the book we have encouraged a focus on connecting – with what matters to you personally as a leader, at the points of interaction where you can have the greatest impact on the organization, and across the organization as a whole. The learning generated at each point of connection can trigger significant challenges to the status quo, and requires a readiness from individual leaders to 'hold the space' long enough for all the differences to emerge and be heard. At the same time we have emphasized the need to rebuild trust – as a way of encouraging institutional confidence, as a way of liberating teams and individuals to act in a way that is both appropriate and timely, and as a means of developing the personal confidence to take decisions and risks that are built on morally sound foundations.

As leaders develop new insights, and are prepared to be different and to learn from their experiences, there will also be a requirement for them to *act* on these touchpoint insights, decisively and openly. This means that leaders need to build practice into their daily and weekly work schedule. This can be as granular as noticing how another person's behaviour triggers a knee-jerk reaction in you, taking a breath before giving an automatic response, or trying out a new conversational approach. Small steps can have a major impact on the way in which a leader's presence is experienced by others – and can help build the agility and courage needed for larger experimentation.

The Touchpoint Leadership developmental framework

Below we provide what we refer to as an inquiry framework to support development across the three Touchpoint Leadership domains. We have included a summary of the developmental framework itself at the end of this section for cross-reference. This is primarily built on a series of questions that we know can catalyse new insights and connections, and assumes the cycles of pause, reflection and new action as we have described it above. It is not a definitive list, and many clients have conducted their own inquiries by building a framework of additional questions that have felt both relevant and generative in their particular contexts. It is not intended as a one-off exercise but is offered as a way of 'being' at the touchpoint, remaining curious and open to experiences, noticing the power of difference, and accepting challenge as an opportunity to evolve and strengthen connections.

Domain 1: Priming the touchpoint to become relational

I wonder whether, if I do not take time out to reflect on what is most important to me and my leadership, I will end up somewhere that I do not want to be... or I will not have left this organization more vibrant than before I came here as leader. (Senior leader)

FIGURE 6.2   Domain 1: Priming the touchpoint

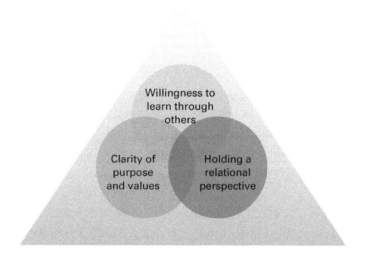

Inquiry framework

Values that create anchors for action

- Reflect on an event in your life that had great emotional impact. How did it feel at the time and what effect did it have on you and your relationships with others? What are your feelings and thoughts now? What does this reflection tell you about what is important to you now?

- Reflect on the events and patterns in your life story and their meaning for you now. What sense of purpose, values and beliefs define you? What assumptions are you carrying about yourself and others? To what extent are your values and beliefs visible to others in the way that you lead? How could you make them more so?

- What makes you *want* to lead – and what makes you not want to lead? What legacy do you want to leave and how does this influence your decisions and actions? How much passion do you feel for your answers?

- Can you articulate the values on which you base your decisions? To what extent do these values define your moral compass – and who else knows that these are your governing principles? How do you know that they serve the collective intent of the business?

Learning with and through others

- How often do you reflect on the vision you originally brought into your leadership role – and make substantial changes to it in the light of experiences or others' perspectives and challenges?

- How much of your time do you devote to enhancing the relationships around you – to enable engagement, teamwork and learning? Do you know how your team and colleagues learn? To what extent are they able to learn from you?

- Of these relationships, which would you describe as comfortable, challenging or bordering on hostile – and how do you react to each of them? How much 'smoothing over' do you do – and to what extent do you value their difference?

- How much time do you spend being the 'expert' in the room – and in what circumstances are you prepared to say you don't have the answers? How vulnerable do you feel when asked that question?

- How curious do you think you are? At the end of today, how much will you have changed in your life – how much will you have learnt and adjusted?

Developing a relational perspective

- How conscious are you of the impact you have in conversations, meetings, discussions? Can you say that others feel liberated and energized by your presence?

- What have you learnt about yourself and how others relate to you? If you were to characterize the kinds of relationships you build, both inside and outside the business, how would you describe them? What sort of feedback is available to you – do you know that this is the most effective you can be?

- What's the single biggest transformation you've achieved in business – and who was key in helping you achieve it?

How would you describe the way in which you relate(d) with them?

- If you were to have access to one more relationship to help you deal with a current and significant challenge what would that give you?

Domain 2: Creating value at the touchpoint

I learnt that if you are disposed to react in certain ways to things, people, events – it is best to create a distance between your reaction and what you do about it. This gives you choice in what you do and say. It doesn't slow you down; it makes you more alive to what is going on. (Senior leader)

FIGURE 6.3   Domain 2: Creating value at the touchpoint

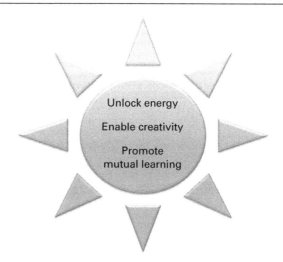

Inquiry framework
Connecting and reinforcing difference

- Which points of connection with others enable you to bring together your different contributions so that you can achieve more than the sum of the parts?

- Which points of connection do you notice where you are intent on getting your own view across regardless of the other's stance, and vice versa?

- How can you help avoid the temptation to smooth over differences in an attempt to integrate them? Or ignore and cover up their existence?

- Look out for the potential for creativity that lies in the difference between people, the frictions or the awkwardness in the room – who is uncomfortable with the tension, who tries to prematurely close down the richness of the potential dialogue?

- Notice polarizing conversations where you get stuck in a see-saw or an either-or debate that is never reconciled. How can you bring this awareness into your meetings and enable others to work with it as a rich source of insight? What deeper question lies underneath the polarity?

- As you look across your colleagues and team, how similar are you all? Are you sure?

- How many 'mavericks' are tolerated in your organization, how often are they rejected or isolated… with what results?

Igniting collective energy

- Notice those relationships that give you energy and those that seem to drain your energy. Pay attention to your own behaviour with these people at the touchpoint. What appears to create energy? What diminishes it? What are you doing to help or hinder the connection?

- Where does the energy seem to spark? Do you know what ignites and sustains it? Does it lead to amazing results? What do you need to do to encourage it?

- When you are in meetings to what extent do you pay attention to what's happening *between* people? Can you map out the repeating patterns that are both helpful and unhelpful?

- Notice your physical and emotional reactions to conversations with others – what tells you that the conversation is triggering you into a response that may be unhelpful?

- Be alert to who seems to be most energized around you, and who seems to lose their spark during conversations and meetings. Can you pinpoint the moment this happens?

- Practise being curious about others' views, needs and perspectives – ask questions for clarification where you would normally not do so.

Catalysing growth and creativity

- Be attentive to the way different people respond to you – how well do you create a climate in which people feel trusted and able to trust you?

- How curious are you in dialogue with others? Do you always know the outcome you need, or can you hold a more open and inquiring mindset?

- Try suspending your immediate responses in meetings and conversations and allow yourself to hear what's behind the words without needing to formulate a response.

- When did a totally different insight emerge in a meeting or conversation – one that took you by surprise, came out of left-field? Could you appreciate its value at the time? What have you missed by holding a firm position that retrospectively you could have relaxed?

- How can you enjoy the ambiguity and complexity – and hold yourself back from rushing to a conclusion or decision?

Domain 3: Building and sustaining the collaborative enterprise

How can we create a connective community of learning that can withstand all the ongoing changes and turmoil, and how do we put our focus on working through our relationships as a means of developing our collective resilience? (Leader in a services firm)

FIGURE 6.4   Domain 3: Building and sustaining the collaborative enterprise

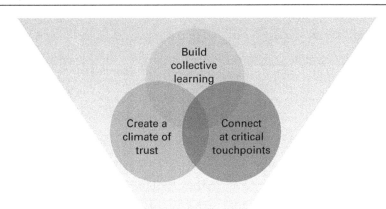

Inquiry framework

Connecting to engage

- To what extent are relationships, and the touchpoint connections they engender, a critical asset to your business?
- Which connections provide most value to the business – and where is most value currently lost? Where do projects break down? Where do departments or divisions underperform?
- What happens when the latest plan or initiative is announced? Who listens for the emotional responses, and especially those that could derail the plans? How do you explore those feelings in a way that transforms that energy into enabling action?
- Which interfaces/touchpoints in the organization are most important to enabling fulfilment of the vision and strategy? How much time do you invest in building and reviewing them? (These can be in the top team, between the top team and the next level of leadership, between departments and divisions, at the interface with clients, customers and suppliers.)
- As you look across your middle leadership population, which relationships seem to have a tremendous impact on their

energy and performance? What can you learn about the quality of these touchpoints and how might you build on those insights to help increase their impact?

- How much time does the leadership team spend on helping *connect* the next generation of leaders: to their own passion for the future, to each other, to the organization, to the client or customer base?

Catalysing connective learning

- Reflect on the major issues facing the business: whose insights does the leadership team currently rely on? Which other connections could render rich insights that are currently unavailable to you? How can you co-create the space in which they can grow and be shared?

- To what extent do the connections in your organization enable true learning? How well do you handle friction at these points of connection?

- How well, as an organization, do you enable people to take risks and learn from mistakes?

- How does information and learning flow across functional and geographic boundaries? Do you hear recurring stories that might indicate that learning is being blocked?

- Which connections are productive and creative? Which seem to get stuck in either-or debates or become polarized around the same, potentially non-viable, options?

- How are the changes and pressures in both the external and internal environment impacting on relationships, and what needs to be addressed?

Trusting to act responsibly and freely

- Can you quantify the level of trust in your organization, and do you know what will help it grow?

- Where is trust being built and where is it being eroded – inside, at the boundaries and outside? What factors are at play and how are you seeking to address them *together*?

- Where do you find yourself trusting enough to lighten control – and where do you seek to increase the control? What is getting in the way? How much are you assuming is 'true' and to what extent have you engaged in dialogue to hear the other possibilities?
- Are there specific points in the organization where silos or organizational layers appear to be stopping collaboration? What is really happening here – what kinds of conversations are happening?
- What do you know about the level of trust at these interfaces? And what needs connecting that is currently disconnected?

FIGURE 6.5   The Touchpoint Leadership developmental framework

Domain 1	Priming the touchpoint to become relational
In priming the touchpoint a leader:	**Key elements:**
Views the challenges of developing Touchpoint Leadership from an individual leader perspective, explores how he personally prepares and develops the capacity for creating the conditions for positive connections with others. Focuses on developing self-awareness, relational agility and a clear moral compass	• Develops a deep appreciation of his own and his organization's purpose and values, and holds himself firmly accountable to these principles • Prepared to be vulnerable in his interactions with others so that he intentionally and consciously grows as a leader • Able to see himself through a relational lens, to discern the patterns that influence his ability to co-create value at the touchpoint
Domain 2	Connecting with others in a way that ignites energy, affirms difference and catalyses co-creation and mutual growth
Igniting connective energy at the touchpoint the leader:	**Key elements:**
Explores what happens at the touchpoint itself, as individuals, teams and groups come together in the spirit of co-creation. This puts the focus on developing a capacity to ignite energy, affirm difference and catalyse mutual growth and which in turn delivers exponential value at the client, team and business partner interfaces	• Affirms the positive qualities of difference in a way that also reinforces the difference – catalysing new insights and connections • Opens up the possibilities for collective action by igniting collective energy at the touchpoint – valuing friction as a rich source of that energy • Catalyses growth and creativity through exchange, trust and mutual learning
Domain 3	Building and sustaining the collaborative enterprise
Co-creating the collaborative enterprise:	**Key elements:**
The touchpoint leader focuses on developing his capacity to engender a culture of learning and collaboration across his organization, taking a systemic view of the connections that need to be made to build collective value. This draws on the capacity of the leader to both identify where the critical connections need to happen and the conditions that need to be present to both sustain and grow them.	• Builds and facilitates connections across the organization as a critical source of engagement and insight • Catalyses connective and sustainable habits of learning that enable the organization to evolve and adapt • Co-creates a climate of mutual trust that enables individuals to act responsibly and freely

Summary

As you reflect on some of these questions we trust that you will also begin to formulate your own – individually and collectively – and use them as a way of drawing people together at the touchpoint in a way that is both generative and catalytic: generative in that it allows new insights to emerge, and catalytic in the way these insights subsequently impact on performance. We would like to encourage leaders to pause before they begin the next restructure, or launch the next change programme, and consider whether it really is through the hard-wiring that they will deliver exponential gains. What if the real efficiencies were to be gained from a capacity to sustain the complex network of relationships and connections that represent the living organization? And what if, by constantly drawing on their insights, you could drive the business forward? Perhaps then we could start to modify the mantra 'change is constant' and instead promote the belief that 'learning is constant', putting the focus on evolving together – organically and healthily – and in a way that individuals are able to deliver with positive energy and freedom for the sake of the business.

Notes

1 For a deeper insight into the key constituents of adult learning see Kolb, D A (1984) *Experiential Learning* (Englewood Cliffs NJ, Prentice Hall).

2 For further insights into this concept of 'restorative energy' see Siegal, D (2007) *The Mindful Brain* (New York, Norton).

3 For deeper guidance on the practice of mindfulness in everyday life, see the work of Jon Kabat-Zinn (2012) *Mindfulness for Beginners: Reclaiming the present moment and your life* and Siegal's work, as in note 2.

4 Other exercises on exploring the 'true' self can be found in McKee, A, Boyatzis, R and Johnston, F E (2008) *Becoming a Resonant Leader: Develop your emotional intelligence, renew your relationships, sustain your effectiveness* (Boston MA, Harvard Business Press).

INDEX

(*italics* indicate a figure or table in the text)